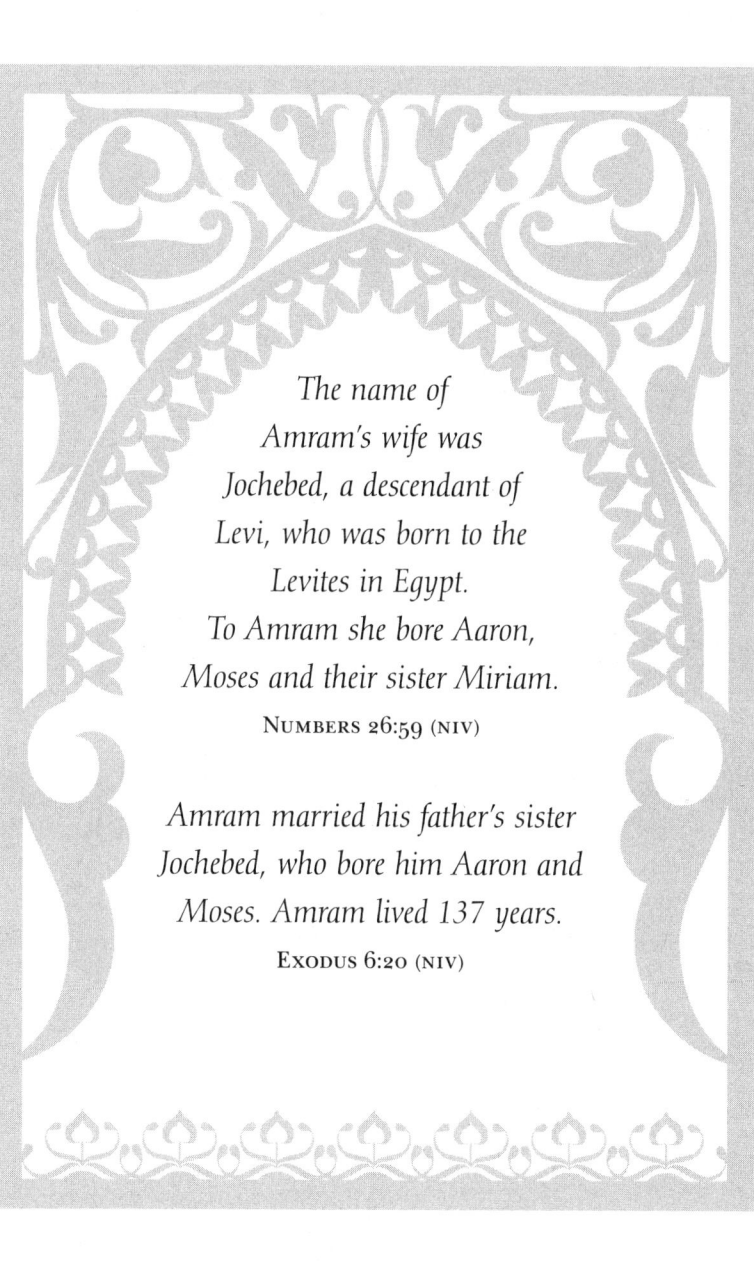

*The name of
Amram's wife was
Jochebed, a descendant of
Levi, who was born to the
Levites in Egypt.
To Amram she bore Aaron,
Moses and their sister Miriam.*

NUMBERS 26:59 (NIV)

*Amram married his father's sister
Jochebed, who bore him Aaron and
Moses. Amram lived 137 years.*

EXODUS 6:20 (NIV)

Ordinary Women of the BIBLE
✦
A MOTHER'S SACRIFICE: JOCHEBED'S STORY

Ordinary Women of the BIBLE

A MOTHER'S SACRIFICE
JOCHEBED'S STORY

CAROLE TOWRISS

Guideposts
New York

Ordinary Women of the Bible is a trademark of Guideposts.

Published by Guideposts Books & Inspirational Media
39 Old Ridgebury Rd.
Danbury, CT 06810
Guideposts.org

Copyright © 2019 by Guideposts. All rights reserved.

This book, or parts thereof, may not be reproduced, stored in a retrieval system, or transmitted in any form or by any means, electronic, mechanical, photocopying, recording, or otherwise, without the written permission of the publisher.

This is a work of fiction. While the characters and settings are drawn from scripture references and historical accounts, apart from the actual people, events, and locales that figure into the fiction narrative, all other names, characters, places, and events are the creation of the author's imagination or are used fictitiously.

Every attempt has been made to credit the sources of copyrighted material used in this book. If any such acknowledgment has been inadvertently omitted or miscredited, receipt of such information would be appreciated.

Scripture references are from the following sources: *New American Standard Bible (NASB)*. Copyright © 1960, 1962, 1963, 1968, 1971, 1972, 1973, 1975, 1977, 1995 by the Lockman Foundation. Used by permission. *The Holy Bible, New International Version (NIV)*. Copyright © 1973, 1978, 1984, 2011 by Biblica, Inc. Used by permission of Zondervan. All rights reserved worldwide. www.zondervan.com. *Holy Bible, New Living Translation*. Copyright © 1996. Used by permission of Tyndale House Publishers, Inc., Wheaton, Illinois 60189. All rights reserved.

Cover and interior design by Müllerhaus

Cover illustration by Brian Call and nonfiction illustrations by Nathalie Beauvois, both represented by Deborah Wolfe, LTD.

Typeset by Aptara, Inc.

Printed and bound in the United States of America

10 9 8 7 6 5 4 3 2 1

Ordinary Women of the BIBLE

✦

A MOTHER'S SACRIFICE

JOCHEBED'S STORY

A special thank-you to astronomer Louis Strous,
who helped me with the "sign" of a comet.
His help was invaluable, but all errors are mine alone.
—Carole Towriss

Cast of CHARACTERS

BIBLICAL

Jochebed/Kebi • birth mother of Mose
Amram • father of Mose
Miriam • sister of Mose
Aaron • brother of Mose
Shiphrah • midwife, mother of Nathanael
Puah • midwife

HISTORICAL

Akhenaten • king who preceded Tutankhamun, father of Tut, Beket, and Ankhe
Beketaten/Beket • princess of Egypt, daughter of Akhenaten, sister of Tutankhamun
Tutankhamun/Tut • king of Egypt
Ankhesenamun/Ankhe • queen of Egypt, half sister and wife of Tutankhamun
Mahu • Chief of Police under Akhenaten (fictional: captain under Tutankhamun, husband of Maia)
Maia • nursemaid of Tutankhamun (fictional: wife of Mahu)

FICTIONAL

Elisheba/Elli • villager
Joel • husband of Elli, Hebrew overseer
Neferet • handmaiden of Beketaten
Benjamin • son of Jochebed and Amram, deceased
Nathanael • son of Shiphrah, friend of Aaron
Hannah • Hebrew handmaiden of Beketaten

Glossary of TERMS

ANCIENT HEBREW

abba • father
ahuvi • beloved, my love (to a male)
ahuvati • beloved, my love (to a female)
El Shaddai • Almighty God (**Shaddai** • The Almighty)
imma • mother
motek • sweetheart

ANCIENT EGYPTIAN

Amun • one of the most powerful gods in ancient Egypt
Aten • the disk of the sun in ancient Egyptian mythology
em hotep • in peace, a greeting or parting phrase
habibi • sweetheart
hemet nesut • queen (literally "royal wife")
kopesh • an ancient sword with a curved blade
Medjay • elite paramilitary police force, bodyguards to king and family, protectors of the king's interests
menat (*pl.* **menatu**) • wet nurse (**menat nesut** • royal wet nurse)
Muut • mother, also the name of an ancient Egyptian goddess
nebet • lady (**nebet-i** • my lady)
nen • no
sa nesut • prince (literally "royal son")
sat nesut • princess (literally "royal daughter")
shabti • funerary figures placed in a tomb to perform tasks for the deceased
shem en hotep • go in peace, goodbye
shenti • linen skirt worn by men
Waset • ancient name for Thebes

INTRODUCTION

The name of Amram's wife was Jochebed, a descendant of Levi, who was born to the Levites in Egypt. To Amram she bore Aaron, Moses and their sister Miriam.

~ Numbers 26:59 (NIV) ~

Amram married his father's sister Jochebed, who bore him Aaron and Moses. Amram lived 137 years.

~ Exodus 6:20 (NIV) ~

The date of the Exodus is one of the most passionately debated topics in all of biblical history. When did it happen? Who was the pharaoh who ordered the murder of the Hebrew baby boys? Who was the pharaoh who refused to allow the Israelites to leave?

And who was the daughter of pharaoh who adopted the infant Moses and raised him as her own?

Scripture gives us none of these names.

There are two generally accepted dates for the Exodus. The early date is approximately 1450 BC, while the late date is approximately 1250 BC.

To determine the Pharaoh of the Oppression, we go back eighty years—forty for the years Moses spent in Egypt and another forty for the years he spent in Midian. For the early

1

date this takes us to Hatshepsut. She had no children and no sisters, so who would be the daughter mentioned in the Moses narrative?

However, eighty years before the late date brings us to 1330 BC. The famous King Tut ruled from 1327–1336.

Tutankhamun had no daughters who survived birth, but he had six (or seven) sisters, all daughters of Pharaoh Akhenaten. Four died before he ascended the throne. One had married and was not heard from after Akhenaten's death. One, his half sister, became his queen.

That leaves Beketaten. Little is known about Beket. Some say she is a daughter of Amen-hotep III and Tiye, making her Tut's aunt. Others say she is a seventh daughter of Akhenaten, with the same mother as Tut—Kiya. For many reasons, this is the theory I find most credible.

It is to this daughter of Pharaoh that Jochebed must entrust the life and soul of baby Moses.

CHAPTER ONE

The king of Egypt said to the Hebrew midwives, whose names were Shiphrah and Puah, "When you are helping the Hebrew women during childbirth on the delivery stool, if you see that the baby is a boy, kill him; but if it is a girl, let her live."

~ Exodus 1:15–16 (NIV) ~

SLAVE VILLAGE OUTSIDE WASET, EGYPT
APEP, THIRD MONTH OF SHEMU, THE HARVEST SEASON, 1330 BC

The lavender hues of dawn glowed through the single window in Jochebed's mud-brick house. The end of another restless night. Expecting her third child, she'd been as ill tempered as a crocodile with her poor husband, Amram.

Too big to climb to the roof, where the air was cooler, she'd slept on the packed dirt floor of their tiny house for many weeks. Though she urged him to join the children, Amram stayed with her. She rolled to her left side and faced him, stretching out her hand to caress his face.

He slept so peacefully, as he did every night after an arduous day's work. She slid her hand down his arm to his hand, coarse and calloused. How could hands so rough and hardened hold her so tenderly?

She hadn't told him, but this pregnancy had been different. The baby hadn't moved as much, hadn't been as active as the others. She hadn't grown as big. The midwives said it wasn't serious enough to concern them, but Jochebed worried.

She winced, feeling a slight tightening low and across her abdomen. She rolled onto her back, thinking a change of position might help—then inhaled sharply and drew up her knees when a hard contraction robbed dawn's peace. She held her breath, waiting for it to pass, and released a slight groan as the births of her other children came to mind.

Amram stirred, his eyes slow to open. A slight smile revealed his lone dimple. "Did you say something, *ahuvati*?"

The contraction ebbed, and a smile played on her lips. She loved it when he called her "my love." How she wished she could let him sleep longer, but the birth of their son Aaron was complete in less than a morning. "Amram, send Miriam to get the midwives."

Her husband was on his feet before his eyes were open, his graying hair skewed in every direction. "Now? Are you all right? When did your pains begin?"

Jochebed accepted his help to stand. "Just send Miriam for the midwives, *ahuvi*." She returned his endearment and pecked his cheek with a kiss. "Perhaps you and little Aaron can stay with me until Miriam returns with Puah and Shiphrah."

"Of course. Yes." He reached the mud-brick steps at the back of the house in five long strides, climbed to the top, and poked his head through the small, square opening in the ceiling. The sound of his whispers filtered down to her as he talked to their seven-year-old daughter.

Moments later, Miriam's bare feet hit the steps, a sleepy smile lighting her features. "I'll be right back, *Imma.*" She patted Jochebed's tummy on her way out of the reed-curtained doorway to fetch Puah, the young midwife, who lived only three doors away. Shiphrah lived five houses north and usually needed to care for her husband and four children before attending a birth.

Thankfully, three-year-old Aaron remained asleep while Amram stoked the cook fire and added water to the barley she'd soaked overnight for their morning meal, then placed that pot over the fire.

Another contraction tore through Jochebed, sending her to one knee. She hoped Puah would bring the birthing bricks to her before going to fetch Shiphrah. The pains were already intense and coming quickly.

Amram knelt beside her and wrapped her shoulders with his strong arm. "Breathe, Kebi. That's what the midwives say, isn't it?"

She nodded, releasing the breath she'd been holding, and tried to inhale and exhale in rhythm with her beloved. He was trembling. This was as hard on him as it was on her. "I've had two easy births and healthy children, Amram. This one will be the same." No need now to tell him of her worries. Or mention Benjamin…

He turned away, sniffled, and nodded his agreement. No words meant his emotions were too raw to speak.

El Shaddai, comfort my Amram.

When Jochebed spent her marriageable years caring for her ailing parents, her older brother showed his gratitude by arranging a marriage with his eldest son—Amram. Though she was nearly too old to be considered a bride by most men, Amram had treated her like a precious treasure from the moment he met her. She knew, however, that he was the gift Shaddai had given her, not the other way around.

Another contraction stole her breath, and Amram shot a concerned look her way. She smiled through gritted teeth.

His warm brown eyes infused her with strength, and she let him lead her to their woven-reed sleeping mat. "I'll sit behind you," he said, leaning against the wall. "You can lie back on my chest until the midwives bring their birthing contraptions."

She leaned back, enduring a few more pains, squeezing her husband's strong hands. He began reciting the sacred, ancient stories, which helped distract them both. Noah's great flood. Abraham's calling. Isaac's love for Rebekah. And Jochebed's favorite: when the Angel of the Lord wrestled with Father Jacob and renamed him *Israel*. Amram's rhythmic voice washed over her, soothing her even when the pains grew more frequent and intense.

Little Miriam rushed through the doorway, tears streaming down rosy cheeks. "Puah is gone. Shiphrah too." Her shoulders shook, and she buried her face in her hands. "I tried to find them, but...they're gone. Just gone."

Behind her, Amram stiffened but said nothing, likely thinking of everything that could go wrong without the midwives' assistance.

When one in three babies did not survive birth, and half of the remaining children did not make it past their first year, his concern was not misplaced.

A Mother's Sacrifice: Jochebed's Story

"Shhh, little one." Kebi called Miriam over with open arms. "It's all right. *Abba* can find them—"

"No!" she shouted, pulling away. "Shiphrah's husband said the king's guards took them as the sun rose. Carried them to the villa in chariots."

Another contraction stole Kebi's voice, but her mind whirred with dreadful possibilities.

Creeping dread began in her arms, prickly and spreading. Then her legs. The birth pain subsided, but the trembling increased. Barely maintaining composure, she spoke quietly to her daughter. "Go back to the roof, Miriam. Stay with your brother until he wakes."

"But I—"

"Go!" She didn't mean to shout. Her daughter looked as if she'd been slapped. "I'm sorry. I need you to go upstairs now." Another pain gripped her, and she bowed her head, biting her bottom lip to keep from crying out.

"Yes, Imma." The sound of Miriam's retreating sandals released Kebi's tears, and panic came in a whisper. "Amram, what if they do not return?"

His arms, like an impenetrable shield, wrapped her in strength, and he pressed his lips against her ear. "You've given birth before. Remember how easy Aaron's birth was?"

Another contraction began. She squeezed her husband's hands, letting out a low groan. Her legs were shaking now, uncontrollably.

7

Amram brushed hair from her forehead, wiping away sweat with it.

Exhaling a long breath after the torturous contraction, Jochebed twisted to face her husband. "This one is different. I haven't told you. I fear something is wrong."

Panic shone in Amram's eyes. "Why would you keep this from me?"

Another contraction rendered Jochebed silent, saving her from offering a less than suitable explanation. A sudden gush of water soaked the reed mat beneath them.

A look of horror on his face, he grabbed her shoulders. "Are you all right? What's happening?" Having always been shooed out of the room, he had no idea what this meant.

She would need to subdue her fear. It would do them no good if they both panicked. She waited for the pain to ebb and framed his face with her hands. "You are going to deliver our child, ahuvi. We'll do it together. All will be well."

Time passed like a desert tortoise—slow but steady.

Miriam tiptoed down the stairs and to the corner of the large common room where the cookware and the dishes waited. She scooped up some of the barley porridge into two bowls for her and Aaron's morning meal and scurried back upstairs. By the time she returned and hastily cleaned the dishes, Kebi felt the overwhelming urge to push. "Get the children out," she said to Amram. "I don't want them to be frightened."

He could only nod, his eyes round as camels' hooves. He called up to his daughter. "Miriam, I want you to get Aaron, take the water jar, and fill it at the river. Then check again to see if the midwives have returned."

As the words were uttered, their doorway curtain stirred, and Shiphrah appeared—then Puah. Kebi blinked to be sure she wasn't dreaming.

"Praise El Shaddai!" Amram nearly leapt to his feet, hurrying to relieve Puah of the birthing bricks. "You're just in time."

Both women's eyes were swollen and red-rimmed. They nudged Amram out of the way but avoided Jochebed's gaze. "Amram, take the children to my house," Shiphrah said. "We'll send word when—" Her voice broke, and she covered a sob.

Puah's face twisted into uncontrolled grief. She tried to turn away, but Kebi grabbed her wrist, pulling her close. "Tell me what's wrong, Puah. Why did they carry you away to the palace?"

Puah avoided Kebi's gaze. "The king called to give us a new order."

Kebi exchanged an anxious glance with Amram. "What kind of order?"

Shiphrah exhaled a deep sigh and stood, meeting Amram's concerned stare. "King Tutankhamun is increasingly under the influence of Vizier Ay—"

"Shiphrah!" Puah glared at her mentor, fire and fear in her eyes. "You should guard your tongue."

"What more can they do to us?" Shiphrah's gaze took in Kebi, then Amram, and then her young friend. "Ay is a wicked, evil man, and he has convinced the king there are far too many Hebrew males, that we are a dangerous people and will one day overthrow him. So the king has ordered us..." Her lips

9

trembled, her voice broke. She looked down at her hands. They were shaking.

Kebi's urge to push overtook her need to hear more, and she cried out. Puah hurried to set up the birthing bricks, while Shiphrah brought in some of the fresh straw they always carried, arranging a thick layer of the dry, tawny stalks around the bricks. "Take the children, Amram." Puah shooed him away, leaning down to hold Jochebed's hand. "We'll care for your wife."

But he stood like a stone in the doorway. "I'm not leaving until you tell me what the king ordered you to do."

Kebi's pain ebbed enough to plead with her friends. "What could the king possibly expect *you* to do to keep him safe?"

The midwives exchanged an uneasy glance, and finally, Puah eyes met Jochebed's. "King Tut ordered us to kill all male Hebrew babies the moment they are born."

Horror strangled Jochebed, and the urge to push silenced her reply. Her body demanded she give life to this child, and searing pain nearly split her in two. For months she'd protected this child within. How could she now deliver it to hands that might harm?

Please, El Shaddai, let this baby be a girl.

Through the open roof of the main room's middle section, Kebi fixed her gaze on the unmoving clouds. This birth was not progressing as easily as Aaron's, and the sun had traveled more than three-quarters of its way across the sky. Squatting on the bricks, her chest heaving, Kebi closed her eyes and leaned back against Puah, who knelt behind her.

Kebi hadn't thought it possible to be this exhausted. It wasn't this hard the other times. It couldn't have been. Piercing pain started low in her belly and snaked through her arms and legs.

Shiphrah looked up. "All right, Kebi. One more huge push, and your baby will be delivered."

Kebi sucked in a breath and bore down, clinging to the image of a baby girl's sweet face.

"The head is out. Keep going! Don't stop now."

Kebi let her breath escape and drew in one more. She leaned forward with fisted hands, then held her breath and pushed with all her might until she felt the infant slide from her body.

"There! You can relax a moment."

Kebi again fell back against Puah, and the young girl dabbed soft cloths on her forehead and neck, wiping away the sweat that had built up over the hours.

"Boy or girl?" Kebi silently ran though the girls' names she and Amram had talked about these last months. Rebekah, Rachel, Netanya, Sarai...

Shiphrah remained silent. The sharp scent of salted olive oil filled the small space. The sounds of gentle rubbing, small whimpers, and Puah's soft voice swirled into a soft but anxious noise.

"Boy or girl?" Kebi repeated.

"Shush, little one." Shiphrah focused only on the babe as she wound strips of fabric around the tiny body.

The tension in the room grew. Maybe they planned to let her discover for herself that Shaddai had blessed them with another girl, allowing relief and joy to flood over her as she held her daughter for the first time.

Miriam would be happy for a sister.

Even as the thought entered her head she knew it was a lie. The child must be a boy, or someone would gladly have told her by now, destroyed the fear that engulfed her.

El Shaddai had given them another son.

But for how long?

Her eyes shot open as Shiphrah placed the babe in her arms. The precious bundle, wrapped securely in wide strips of old tunic from neck to tiny toes, blinked once at her and slipped into sleep.

He was perfect. So utterly beautiful. A soft pink to his cheeks. Dark, wet curls plastered to his forehead. Red lips, slightly parted, the top one in the shape of a bow.

She untucked the swaddling the midwife had so carefully wrapped him in to expose tiny hands, clasped at his chest.

She pried open his fingers, counting them. Ten.

She unwrapped further.

Five toes on one foot, five on the other.

And yes, he was a boy.

Vision blurred, she wrapped him again.

He squirmed, a small cry escaping his lungs.

Keeping one arm under him, with her free hand she gently grasped his head, turning it toward her breast.

He squirmed more. She pressed his mouth against her skin. After several attempts, he found his place and began suckling.

Kebi had always loved feeding her babies. For those moments, nothing else existed but her and her infant. She had to stop cleaning, cooking, grinding grain—there was no more important job on earth than providing nourishment to one so utterly dependent on others. El Shaddai must have designed it this way so mothers would stop and focus on nothing else, giving their children the love that was as essential to their survival as milk.

A slight pain in her breast brought to mind the pain she endured before...when Benjamin, born before Aaron, did not survive past a quarter year. The pain as her milk slowly dried up...as her breasts became engorged with milk no child would ever drink.

Surely Shaddai would not take another child from her.

He wouldn't, would He?

The baby suckled, soothing not only himself but her as well. *The baby.* He needed a name.

But would it be harder or easier to deal with his absence if she had a name to cling to?

Without a name, would it be simpler to forget him, let him slip into obscurity? Forget the devastating loss?

Even without a name she would never forget him.

He needed a name—or rather, she needed one—that would remind her to trust in the Almighty in the face of death. "We will call him Tovyah."

Shiphrah smiled. "*God is good.* I like it."

"What are you going to do?" Puah's soft voice drifted over her shoulder.

"I don't know yet." Her voice broke.

"Let's concentrate on keeping this one safe for now, all right?" Shiphrah drew a damp cloth over Kebi's face, wiping away the sweat and tears. "*We* certainly aren't going to hurt him. Let's get a fresh tunic on you."

Kebi allowed him to nestle into Shiphrah's arms, then relaxed a bit while Puah changed her garment and gently but thoroughly cleaned her from head to toe with cloths dipped into a large bowl of water.

"Feel better now?" Shiphrah forced a smile.

"Not really."

"I know," Shiphrah whispered as she returned the infant to his mother.

Kebi pushed the king and his edict from her mind. Only Shaddai knew for certain what would happen. Worrying about it wouldn't change anything.

For now, there was only her newborn son.

CHAPTER TWO

Then Pharaoh gave this order to all his people: "Every Hebrew boy that is born you must throw into the Nile, but let every girl live."
~ Exodus 1:22 (NIV) ~

MESUT-RA, FOURTH MONTH OF SHEMU, THE HARVEST SEASON

Kebi sat up and tied her sash around her waist again. Shiphrah washed her hands in a bowl of water and reached for a cloth. "Everything seems to be progressing well. You'll bleed for several more weeks, and then your body will go back to normal."

Kebi grinned. "I remember."

"Of course you do. I'm sorry. I've cared for several new mothers lately, and I've become used to explaining everything in detail."

Kebi glanced at Tovyah sleeping peacefully next to her. "Are many babies being born?"

"About the same as usual."

"And are they...safe?"

"So far." She pursed her lips. "The king called us back again yesterday."

"What did he want?"

"He wanted to know why none of the babies born yet have been killed."

"What did you tell him?"

"I told him that the Israelite mothers are stronger than the Egyptian women. That they are delivered before we can even get there."

"Did he believe you?"

"I think so. Most men know so little about women they'll believe anything you tell them." She laughed dryly.

Kebi paused, afraid to ask the question that had consumed her thoughts these last days. "Has anyone lost their son yet?"

"Not here. I heard that in other villages some were lost."

"Do you know any more about why the king gave such an order in the first place?"

"It appears that the royal astrologers told him of an ancient prophecy that predicted the birth of an Israelite boy who would eventually overthrow the Egyptians. The birth would occur when a long-tailed star appeared in the sky. The night before Tovyah was born, they saw the star low in the south. They woke the king and informed him that the prophecy was about to be fulfilled. He immediately called us and ordered that all male babies be killed so this usurper would never live."

"And how long will this order last?"

"Until the star can no longer be seen." She paused, intent on drying hands that were no longer wet. "They think it will leave before the Nile floods again."

Jochebed counted off the months. "That's…two more months." Her hope evaporated like steam rising from barley stew. She could never keep Tovyah quiet for such a long time. At some point, she would have to do something.

But what?

In the dark of night, Kebi's eyes shot open. She groaned. Her dream had been so sweet. Why must she awaken to such miserable thoughts?

She'd been able to hide Tovyah for a month. Keeping him close, she fed him at the slightest whimper. If she slept soundly, which was rare, his cries at night were obscured by the whimpering growls of the hyenas and the barking of the jackals that prowled outside the village walls.

Amram rolled to face her. "Are you awake?"

"I am now." She released a long sigh. "What are we going to do?"

He scrubbed a hand down his face. "Well, let's think about this. One, we do nothing and hope they don't find him. Two, we let them take him now, before he is found by them, and pray for mercy for him and for us and for Shiphrah and Puah, who allowed him to live."

"Do you really think they'd be punished? We can tell them they didn't arrive in time."

"That excuse doesn't work anymore. The king has decreed *all* Egyptians are to throw any newborn boys into the river."

"All of them? Anyone who knows of one?" Kebi rose up on her elbow.

"Anyone. Anyone living in Waset."

"When did he say that?"

"Yesterday."

"Why didn't you tell me?"

"What difference would it have made? I didn't want to cause you pain for no reason."

She dropped back to the mat. "Thank you. I guess."

Amram rose up on one elbow. "Three, we allow him to join our ancestors in a more peaceful fashion."

"What?" Her voice squeaked as she tried to keep the horror that washed over her from waking Tovyah.

"I'm just wondering if dying in our arms, loved and wanted, isn't better than being thrown to crocodiles, hated and feared."

She lay down again, rolling to face the wall. "I can't believe you even said that."

He placed a hand on her arm. "Kebi, turn over."

She remained still.

"Kebi, look at me."

She rolled back to place her shoulders flat on the ground but kept her knees pointed away from him. "You really want us to—"

"Of course I don't want us to do that. I'm just trying to think of every possible option, saying whatever comes to mind. Sometimes that helps bring up other things we haven't thought of."

"I don't like any of those choices. I cannot lose another baby." The picture of Benjamin's sweet but still face refused to leave her mind.

"Neither do I. But I can't think of anything else."

"We could hide him."

"Hide him? How do you hide a baby? They cry, they squirm, sometimes they smell…"

She tried to suppress the laughter that bubbled up. Apparently unsuccessfully.

"I wasn't trying to be funny."

"I know, ahuvi. I'm sorry." Her voice dropped to a whisper. "I can't let them take him. I just… I can't lose another baby." Her throat burned as the tears welled. She drew in a deep breath. She couldn't cry. He'd think her too emotional to be reasonable, dismiss everything she said if her words were accompanied by tears. "Give me six months with him. Let me hold him and pray for him and feed him for a little longer."

His strong hand cupped her face. "I don't think of five months as a 'little longer.' Every day we keep him we are all in danger. The king could have all of us killed."

"Then what do you want me to do?" She tried to steady her voice, but still it broke.

He lay back down, his hand under his head. "I don't know, ahuvati. Let's keep praying. Perhaps El Shaddai will send the answer."

She moved nearer to him and placed her head on his chest. He slid his arm around her and pulled her close.

If Shaddai was going to send an answer, He had better do it quickly.

She wasn't going to count on Him, though. He hadn't done much so far.

Morning broke early. Jochebed rubbed the sleep from her eyes. Neither of them had slept much after their discussion in the darkest hours of night. A conversation that yielded no answers, no plan.

Amram sat beside her, elbows on knees, staring at the wall. How long had he been awake?

She reached up to rub his back. "Is everything all right?"

"I… I had a dream." He spoke but remained still.

She sat up and turned to face him. "What kind of dream?"

"Shaddai sent an angel to talk to me."

Kebi resisted scoffing. El Shaddai sent angels to important people—Abraham and Sarah. Jacob. Lot. Not slaves in the desert. God hadn't sent a messenger to anyone in Egypt since Joseph brought them here. Perhaps He had forgotten them.

Of course she would never say that aloud. "What did the angel say?"

"He said our son is a very special one and that we must do all we can to protect him. He said…" His voice drifted off as he dropped his head onto his arms.

She touched his arm. "What? What did he say?"

Amram answered, but his words were garbled.

"What? I can't understand you when you talk to the floor."

He raised his head. "He said Tovyah will grow up to free our people from their bondage."

"Our son? This little baby, right here?" Kebi cupped Amram's cheek and turned his head to face her. "Are you sure you heard correctly? Neither of us has had much sleep these last few weeks."

"I heard correctly." His gaze locked on hers. "He said it three times...because I wouldn't believe him."

She held up her hands in surrender. "All right." It was clear he fervently believed what he was saying, even if she did not.

"He said something else."

"What's that?"

"He said that everything we teach Tovyah, he will remember when it is time."

"What does that mean?"

He shrugged. "I'm not sure. He said we would have to let him go for him to carry out God's plan but that the words of Shaddai would return to his heart when he needed them."

"What plan? What does 'let him go' mean? How will the words 'return to his heart'? Did he say when that would happen? When will it be time?" So many questions clamored for answers.

"He didn't say."

"What are we supposed to do with that? That's almost worse than telling us nothing!" She tried to keep any bitterness from her voice.

"Be careful, Jochebed, how you treat the words of El Shaddai."

He rarely called her by her full name. "I'm sorry." She wasn't, really, but he would shut down altogether and stop talking if she didn't say it. "But really, how does this help us?"

"I guess we need to try to teach him whatever we can about El Shaddai before..."

She ignored his implication. "He's a newborn babe. Do you think he understands a word we say?"

"I don't know. But we must obey whether we think so or not." He stood and headed for the open-roofed cooking area at the back of the house.

She scrambled up and followed.

As he did every morning before he left, Amram squatted before the firepit, poking at it with a long, thick stick. Embers flying, bringing the flames back to life.

"Amram!"

He looked up over his shoulder, brows furrowed. "What?"

What? How could he say everything he'd said and act as if he'd told her he'd like another piece of bread? "You know what. What makes you think I will ever let them take him from me?"

He returned his attention to the embers, coaxing them back to life. "El Shaddai said we must."

She huffed. "They'll have to pry him away from me. I can't just hand him over knowing they will…"

"No, they won't."

"How do you know that?"

"El Shaddai has told us he will grow up to lead Israel out of bondage. He has to live to do that. I don't know how, and it doesn't matter whether we like it or not."

A whimper drew her attention to Tovyah. She stepped back to her mat and picked up her son, who buried his face in her tunic, his mouth open and searching. She loosened the tie at her neck and helped him settle in for his first meal of the day.

When it is time. What was she supposed to do with that?

For now she'd ignore it. It didn't matter anyway. Because Tovyah was staying right here.

No matter what anyone said.

The sound of neighing horses and chariot wheels destroyed the village's midmorning calm. Sandals pounded sandy streets intent on ridding Egypt of anything—no matter how small—that might prove a threat to their king.

Israelites who only a moment before sat peacefully in their doorways watching small children play and chatting among themselves burst into action. Children paralyzed by fear squealed and stood still as statues, hands over eyes, trying to blot out the horrible sight. Mothers dragged them back inside, pulling their doors down.

Kebi jumped to her feet. She'd kept Tovyah safe from the prying eyes of villagers, but that wouldn't be enough to protect him from the *Medjay*. The elite guards selected to protect king and palace would stop at nothing to complete their task.

Miriam raced into the room from outside, Aaron close behind her.

Kebi tossed aside the tunic she'd been mending and retrieved Tovyah from the blanket he lay upon. "Quick! You know what to do."

Her face set with grim determination, Miriam stretched out her short arms to receive him. She crushed him against her chest, wrapped her outer garment around him, and turned to dart out the back, almost in one smooth motion.

Since they had learned of the king's new edict, Kebi and her daughter had developed a dangerous plan to keep Tovyah safe. At the first sign of the Medjay, Miriam would tuck her baby brother under her cloak and race to hide with him in the tall papyrus reeds that lined the river. With the water nearly at its lowest point of the year, most of the reeds weren't in standing water but merely in mud.

Thank Shaddai they lived near the eastern gate of their village, closest to the river.

Kebi watched from the opening until she could no longer see Miriam, then crept back through the common room to the door. She pulled the curtain from the doorway, just enough to see the street crawling with hateful guards.

The Medjay showed up without warning every five or six days. This time, they showed up two days in a row, counting on complacency setting in. Their gamble paid off.

Assuming the guards would not return so soon, many mothers had brought their sons into the fresh air, in plain view.

Kebi pressed her palms to her ears, but nothing could keep out the shrieking and begging that flooded the village.

At the far end of the street, a young mother raced out her door and ran toward the gate, a newborn in her arms.

The Medjay didn't bother chasing her. One of them calmly reached for the small of his back and retrieved an arrow from the quiver hanging from his shoulder. He nocked it, pulled, and released. Her back arched and arms flew wide as the missile hit her squarely. Blood soaked the back of her tunic as she fell facedown into the sand. Another guard retrieved the squalling babe.

The men continued marching down the street.

Kebi backed away from the door and scurried to the other side of the room. Huddled against the wall, she prayed.

El Shaddai, God of Abraham, Isaac, and Jacob, protect my children. Grant Miriam wisdom as she hides near the river with my son. Blind the eyes of those who seek to destroy him. Keep them safe.

Aaron tugged on her tunic. She glanced down. His wide brown eyes melted her heart, and she bent to gather him in her arms.

Kebi jumped as the door swished. Aaron whimpered and buried his face in her chest.

A guard stepped through, his massive form dwarfing their house. His broad shoulders grazed the doorposts. Skin glistening with sweat, bow over his shoulder, quiver at his side, he grasped a short bronze ax in his hand—the favorite weapon of the Nubian Medjay.

He glared at Kebi, dark eyes peering from a scowling face. His ebony chest contrasted with the bright white of the linen *shenti* around his waist. The kilt reached to just above his knees and was held in place by a thin strip of linen tied at his waist.

He stomped toward the cooking area. Peering out the narrow doorway, he scanned the pots and jars, none big enough to conceal a baby. On his way back, he used his ax to flip the top off a basket containing their newly cleaned tunics and cloaks. Seeing only fabric, he kicked it. It toppled over, spilling out its contents. He grunted and left, the door flapping in his wake.

Sliding to the ground, Kebi released the breath she'd been holding.

Thank You, Shaddai. Once again, they had evaded the guards.

Anguished screams from the house across the street brought an abrupt end to her relief. She jumped up and ran to the door to peer out. One of the Medjay dragged Elisheba from her house by one arm, her other cradling a newborn close to her chest. Both hands around the infant's torso, he pulled at the screaming child until he freed him from his mother's embrace.

Kebi covered her mouth to stifle the sob that welled up within her. Losing a son was bad enough—but having him pried from your arms by force... The pain was unimaginable.

"It's either him or *both* of you!" The guard's voice echoed down the street, now deserted. No one, parent or not, wanted to be witness to this display of Egyptian cruelty.

Kebi didn't want to watch either, but she couldn't look away.

Marching toward the river, the guard dangled the babe by one arm like a discarded doll. When Elisheba grasped the edge of his shenti, he turned slightly and smacked her arm away with the handle of his ax.

The bereft mother crumbled to the ground, her sobs depriving her of all strength. Only for a moment. Elisheba scrambled to her feet, running after the Medjay.

Kebi closed her door, Elisheba's shrieks ringing in her ears. She pulled Aaron close, burying her face in his neck.

Why, El Shaddai? Why?

CHAPTER THREE

✦

When she saw that he was a fine child, she hid him for three months. But when she could hide him no longer, she got a papyrus basket for him and coated it with tar and pitch.
~ Exodus 2:2–3 (NIV) ~

DYEHUTY, FIRST MONTH OF AKHET, THE SEASON OF INUNDATION

A soft whimper followed by squirming at her side signaled to Kebi that Tovyah was awake and ready to be fed. She rolled on her side. Within moments he was contentedly suckling, and the only sound in the darkened mud-brick house was his swallowing.

For over two months she had managed to hide her son from the king's marauders. She wore him close to her heart, secured by a long piece of fabric. Only when she knelt near the river to wash their clothes did she leave him at home, making sure he was satisfied and sleepy before she left him with Miriam. Even then she was never gone for long.

"My sweet boy." She drew her fingers over his cheek. How could she possibly protect him? *If a child isn't safe with his mother, then where can he be safe?*

No matter what happened, she wanted him to know about El Shaddai. To know he was one of Shaddai's people.

"Do you know that El Shaddai created you?" she whispered. "Our father Abraham left his father's home and traveled to a land Shaddai had promised him. God said He would make of Abraham a great nation, that He would bless him and make his name great. Abraham had Isaac, Isaac had Jacob, and Jacob had twelve sons. And for hundreds of years they lived happily in the land and worshipped El Shaddai.

"Then one day ten of the brothers sold one of the youngest as a slave, because they were jealous of him. He was brought here to Egypt, and he became a ruler of this land."

How far they had fallen!

Tovyah's gaze held hers as she recited the story, as if drinking in her words along with her milk. "But over the years, we lost our favor with the king. A new king forced us to work as slaves instead. We toil and we struggle and we wait for El Shaddai to return us to the land He promised us."

How long that would be was anyone's guess.

Tovyah drifted back to sleep, and she rolled onto her back. The space beside her was empty. Amram must have left for the brickfields.

Miriam appeared on the steps, Aaron behind her. She padded over and knelt beside her baby brother. "Good morning, Imma. Good morning, Tovyah." She gently rubbed his head.

Kebi sat up. "Miriam, will you watch your brother so I can go down to the river?"

"Of course, Imma. Watch out for the crocodiles."

Kebi smiled as she stood. "I will." At the little table out back, she poured a tiny bit of water into her hands, then washed her face. Grabbing a head scarf on her way out, she glanced back once more at Miriam, who had curled her small body around her brother's on the mat, Aaron on his other side.

Kebi strolled to the river. What was she going to do? Even if she could hide him for the six months she had asked of Amram, then what? It would be obvious to any Egyptian that entered the village that he had been born during the time of the long-tailed star. And that would be the end for all of them.

She glanced up. The fuzzy green star with a long, shiny white tail was setting in the southeast after its nightly trek across the sky. Each night its path moved farther north, and if it kept the same pace, would indeed disappear by the time the Nile inundated now-dead fields.

Kebi stepped into the shallow water, first checking for the man-eating crocodiles. Only a few of the smaller, friendly ones swam nearby. The dangerous ones spent most of their day on the sandbars in the middle of the river, basking in the sun.

A large grouping of bulrushes grew a few steps downriver from where she stood. Her feet disappearing into the squishy mud, she made her way toward the plants. Reaching down, she yanked them out by the roots, tossing them onto a pile on the bank.

Laughter—a sound not often heard in the village recently—sounded. A group of women, Egyptians by their dress, laughed and teased each other as they washed clothes. Though under the king's control and subject to be summoned at any moment to do his bidding, however trivial, they were still free.

At this moment she envied them.

A small boy ran toward the group and hopped on his mother's back, wrapping his arms around her neck as she bent over her task. Laughing, she turned her face to kiss him, and he ran off, giggling.

The women, except for one, laughed with her. Younger than the others, her face held a pained smile until the child darted off.

Kebi knew well what she must be feeling. Two agonizing years had passed after her marriage before she had conceived Miriam. Every month she'd been reminded of her failure as a woman. Happy mothers with cooing babies had made her sick to her stomach, and she'd avoided them whenever possible. An almost physical pain had engulfed her when she was forced to be around them.

What if...

No. The thought was too outrageous.

Israelite babies belonged with Israelite mothers. She would think of something else.

Although she'd been thinking for a month and had come up with nothing better.

◆

Each arm clutching a jug of water, Kebi trudged from the river toward home.

Her heart broke at the sight of Elisheba shuffling toward her, steps heavy, shoulders slumped, unrelenting sorrow etched into her face.

Kebi halted. "Elli, I am so sorry—"

"Sorry? What good does sorry do for me? My son is dead." Her face twisted into an agony-filled grimace and then into a suspicious glare. "Why do you look so calm? Your baby was due the same time as mine was. What happened to him?"

"She is a girl." The words left her mouth before her mind could pull them back. Why had she lied? Eventually the truth would be known throughout the village, whatever happened, and her word would no longer be trusted.

Elli narrowed her eyes. "No." Her voice was calm, but the rage that lurked below was unmistakable. "If you had delivered a girl, you would have danced in the street. I know I would have." She scowled, slowly nodding. "No, you had a boy."

Kebi glanced around. No one was in sight. She could never admit now her baby was a boy. If Elli's anger was unleashed…

There was nothing to be done now except continue the lie. "I had a girl."

"Then you must show her to me so I can rejoice with you." Her smile told Kebi rejoicing was the last thing on Elli's mind.

"No!" Kebi's heart raced as she took three large steps toward her door. "She's sleeping, and I don't want to awaken her. Perhaps when she is older. She is so very small."

"I don't believe you."

"I can't really help what you believe.…"

Elli neared her again. "I'll find out. Then I will tell the Egyptians. And then we'll see what happens to your precious son—and to you."

Kebi cringed. It wasn't her fault Elisheba's baby was dead. She could have tried harder, hid him as Kebi had. And even if not, how could she blame Kebi when it was the Egyptians who had thrown Elli's baby into the Nile?

She had protected him this long. She would not let a grieving, jealous mother ruin it now. She would fight to keep him safe, away from anyone who threatened him, whether Israelite or Egyptian. "You will not come near me, or anyone in our family, do you understand?" Her lowered voice reminded her of the growl of a lion robbed of her cubs. "What do you think the Egyptians will do if you tell them I have a boy, and they discover I have a girl? How do you think they will react to your wasting their time?"

The scowl disappeared from Elli's face, replaced by the slightest of smiles. "I don't know. Maybe it would be worth it, worth whatever they do to me. I have nothing to live for now."

How could she say that? "You have five other children! Living children who need you."

She scoffed. "Daughters! They'd be better off without me."

Kebi set her water jugs in the soft earth beside the reed bundle that served as a doorframe, then turned to stretch a hand toward the woman. When she didn't retreat, Kebi stepped near enough to touch her arm. "Elisheba, what happened? We were friends."

She jerked back. "We *were*. We are not now. I have no friends. Nothing except my grief to keep me warm." Her voice drifted off, replaced by a choking sob. "Joel won't touch me. He thinks I am at fault for allowing them to take our son."

"I'm sure that will pass. He is suffering as much as you are. Elli, you can't let grief rob you of everything, of the rest of your life."

Her face hardened again, her glare drilling into Kebi. "You try living after your child has been eaten by a crocodile. It can't be done." She turned on her heel and stomped toward the river.

Kebi stared at Elli's retreating figure.

Was Elli right? How would Kebi react if—*when*—she finally lost Tovyah? Would she take it out on those around her, those whom she now loved? She'd already lied. What would deception lead to?

El Shaddai, guard my heart. Keep me from allowing sorrow, or fear, to harden it.

She'd need His help. Judging by what she had just done, she wouldn't be able to do it on her own.

◆

The sky was still a grubby gray, dawn's beautiful pinks and purples not yet awake.

Inside their house, the mood was not any brighter.

Kebi tried to avoid her husband's gaze.

"This can't go on. Look at you. Your tunic hangs on you like it was made for a woman twice your size. You spend all your time listening for the Medjay. You keep Tovyah closer to you than your own breath." Amram wrapped his hands gently around her upper arms and pulled her closer. "You don't eat.

You don't sleep. You avoid everyone outside of our home. You're cross and irritable. Shaddai said *we* are to teach him, but you won't let me near him. This is no good for any of us."

"What do you suggest I do? I have to keep him hidden. If it becomes known now that we have an almost-three-month-old boy, the other villagers will retaliate. Which won't matter, because the Egyptians will kill us all."

"I think most of the village knows we have a baby boy."

"But we have the only baby who has not yet been found. And turned into a snack for the crocodiles." Kebi sighed. "And I need to go to the river before they awaken. I have to wash Aaron's tunic and get some flax…"

"Let me do it."

She laughed dryly. "*You* will wash the clothes?"

He smirked. "Perhaps not. But I can take care of Tovyah while you do it."

Heat flooded her face. Had she really kept Tovyah so fiercely to herself? Away from his own father? "I'm so sorry I've kept him from you." She loosened the knot on the shawl that held him to her chest, then slid the babe into his father's arms.

"Are you sure?"

She nodded. "You both need this. He's just been fed, and I won't be long."

A warm peace flooded her as one corner of Amram's mouth turned up. She hadn't seen his reassuring smile for far too long.

"He has your eyes," Amram said.

She waved a hand. "He's much too little to decide that yet."

"No, he's not. I could see you in Miriam and Aaron as soon as they were born. She has your nose, and he has your smile."

"If you say so. I should go, so I can get back. Joel will be pounding on the doorframe soon."

"His new position as supervisor has made him proud. And nearly unbearable."

She dropped a kiss on Tovyah's head. "I'll hurry."

"Mm-hmm," Amram murmured.

Kebi pulled aside the reed curtain, casting a last glance at Amram gazing at his son. She'd always known saying goodbye to Tovyah would rip her heart to shreds, but she was ashamed to admit she'd never given much thought to how Amram would feel, let alone Miriam and Aaron.

Had she just made it harder for her husband?

CHAPTER FOUR

❖

Then she placed the child in it and put it among the reeds along the bank of the Nile. His sister stood at a distance to see what would happen to him.
~ Exodus 2:3–4 (NIV) ~

PAENIPAT, SECOND MONTH OF AKHET, THE SEASON OF INUNDATION

Kebi adjusted the sling that wrapped over her left shoulder and then around her right side to keep Tovyah cradled against her back. For the first time, she had brought him with her to the river. His soft coos told her he was awake and content.

In shin-deep water, Kebi wrapped her fist around the bottom of a bulrush and yanked one of the three-sided plants from the mud. Rising far over her head, the stems were much too tall to be carried without cutting them into smaller pieces. She pulled a small blade from deep within her sash to slice them in thirds before she placed the pieces into a basket.

The Egyptian mothers she had seen so often knelt in the shallow water of the Nile.

A silent prayer snaked through her thoughts, and she reached behind her to pat Tovyah's leg.

El Shaddai, please give one of them a heart for my son.

She'd resisted the idea for weeks now, since the first time she saw them.

It kept returning.

Kebi ignored their conversation, their giggles, their children, harvesting the towering rushes until she collected an orderly pile. Gathering them into a bunch, she wrapped her arm around it, hoisting the reeds onto her right shoulder, taking care to keep the back end high over Tovyah's head. Her left hand against it to keep it steady, she plodded toward home.

After shoving the door open with the ends of the reeds, she laid her cargo on the floor against the wall before pouring herself some water.

She twisted the sling to her chest. Supporting the baby with one hand, she unknotted the sling with the other. The rhythmic swaying as she walked home had lulled Tovyah to sleep, and she carefully placed him on a straw-stuffed reed mat to finish his morning nap, then sat beside him.

Knife in one hand, stalk in the other, she made a small slit along the juncture between two of the plant's three sides. She poked the knife through and out the adjacent juncture, then slid the knife to the end, releasing one of the peels. She did the same for all three sides. When she was done she had three long strips of strong, flexible reed that could be used to make sandals, pots, doors, and baskets, among other things. She picked up another and repeated the process, over and over.

The sound of neighing horses and pounding feet sent a chill through her body. Where was Miriam? No matter, wherever she was she could never get back in time to take Tovyah to the river.

Kebi had come this far. She couldn't let the Egyptians take him from her. Not now.

She jumped to her feet, her heart pounding in her ears. Screaming in the street made it nearly impossible to come up with a plan. *Think. Think!*

The roof was no good. They'd climbed up there before. She looked toward the cooking area. Nothing big enough to hide him in. And if he awoke and began to cry—then what?

El Shaddai, help me!

The footsteps drew nearer. There was only one option, and not a very good one. The lightweight plants were stacked around the sleeping infant, the peeled outsides on top of him, just enough to hide the brightly colored tunic he wore. She left small air spaces for him to breathe. Thank Shaddai he was a sound sleeper.

She sat beside him and picked up her knife again, trying to control her breathing. If the guard realized she was nervous, he would suspect something. Search even harder.

She removed one side of a plant and turned to place it on top of the pile spread over Tovyah. Then she saw it.

A corner of bright blue fabric peeking through the reeds. She reached to poke it back in place when a Medjay burst through the door.

The man's olive skin told her he was one of the highest-level guards. Only Egyptians were allowed to guard the king and his family, to occupy the office of Greatest of the Medjay. The guard stomped through to the back, scanning the room. He stared at the pile of papyrus for a long, heart-stopping moment.

His careworn gaze caught hers, held it.

Then he stomped out.

Kebi let out a long breath of relief.

Did he not see the indigo cloth peeking out between the reeds? She rose to stand where he had stood to see if it was visible. Rose up on her toes. He was much taller than she was, but the taller she stood, the more visible it was.

He had to have seen it. Did he not care? Perhaps he'd had enough of throwing helpless, howling infants into the toothsome jaws of river monsters.

Did he feel sorry for her? Show mercy? Doubtful. Everyone knew the Medjay were fearless, merciless.

It had to be the work of El Shaddai. There was no other answer.

She could deny the obvious no longer. The realization of what she needed to do finally found a home in her heart. As difficult as it would be, helplessly watching him murdered before her eyes would be infinitely harder.

Determination exploded in her chest. There was no more time. She had to finish, tonight. She'd stay awake all night if that's what it took. Perhaps Amram and even Miriam could help.

But whatever it took, Tovyah couldn't be here the next time the king's guards visited the village.

Not if she wanted to keep him alive.

The oil lamp flickered at her side, casting just enough light for Kebi to weave reeds in and out, around and through each other. She looked at the Tovyah-sized basket she'd completed. It was her finest work ever.

She'd made sure of that.

The sound of heavy footfalls on the mud-brick steps drew her attention. She glanced up but continued weaving the long pieces of reed into a circle.

Amram came to sit by her. "You never came up. Did you sleep at all?" He stretched a hand toward Tov, sleeping beside her. He stopped just short of touching him.

"I couldn't sleep."

"It's no wonder. It's so hot and stuffy down here. Why won't you come to the roof with the rest of us?"

She shrugged. "I don't want to take the chance. I can't hide him up there."

He fingered the edge of the basket. "I thought we finished this last night. After I coated it with pitch."

She turned the reed circle in her hands. "He needs a covering. The sun is so hot…who knows how long it will take before someone finds him?"

He leaned in and kissed her cheek. "You are an excellent imma." He stood and reached for a clean tunic. At least as clean as she could get it. Even though he often shed it when he piled mud and straw into brick molds, it came home every day caked in red mud.

"Is it time for you to go?"

"Yes. Are you doing this today?"

"I have to. I can't risk what happened yesterday happening again." She paused. "Thank you for covering the basket with pitch."

He nodded and headed for the door.

"Do you want to hold him? Say goodbye?"

Amram reached for the door. "I don't know. Maybe it's best I don't." His voice was choked.

"Think about a year from now. Will you wish you'd held him one last time?"

He dropped his head. Maybe she shouldn't push. He was never very good with strong emotions. She needed to give him a graceful way out of the trap she'd just led him into, even if she hadn't meant to. "Or would you rather your last memory be a happy one? That's all right too."

He slipped out the door without looking at them again.

She understood. When overwhelmed, he always went silent. When he held his children the first time. When she agreed to marry him. When his father was killed.

The door opened again, slowly. Amram neared her, knelt before them.

"I need to say goodbye," he whispered.

He took Tovyah from his place beside her, then stood again.

Tovyah looked so small, so fragile against Amram's broad chest. Amram's strong arms, muscled and brown from a lifetime of making thousands upon thousands of bricks, held the fragile body of his son close. He began to pace as he whispered. She'd give anything to know what he said, but his words were meant only for his son's ears.

Every so often, she heard him mention El Shaddai. Was he praying for him?

Probably. Amram prayed often. For everything. Kebi prayed each morning, and before she drifted off to sleep, but usually no more. It seemed as though when Amram wasn't talking to anyone else, he prayed.

The noises outside were slowing. If he didn't leave soon, he'd be late. Joel would come for him, and that meant a lashing, from him or one of the other Israelite foremen, who often took their jobs far too seriously just to gain a little extra grain each month.

Amram stopped his pacing. He buried his face in Tovyah's neck for a long moment, then turned his head to kiss his cheek. He laid the child in Kebi's lap, then hurried out the door without looking back.

◆

As her son suckled for the last time, Kebi's eyes traced the curves of his face, committing each feature to memory. His hands were clasped at his chest, his eyes locked on hers. Did he somehow know what she was planning to do?

"You do know this is not because I don't love you, don't you? It's because I love you more than breath." Her voice broke. "I would give my life if it would protect you. Without a second thought. But it wouldn't stop those who are bent on hurting you, and I cannot bear to see harm come to you. Even if I must give you to another." Her tears rolled down her cheeks, landing on her tunic, her arm…his face.

"El Shaddai, protect my son. Keep him safe from crocodiles, hippos, and barques. Keep him close to the bank until he finds the one who will love him. May she welcome him with open arms and give him the care I cannot. Don't let the false gods of Egypt fill his heart and turn him from You, Almighty God. I know he will probably not remember the mother who gave him life, but somehow let him come to know You." Sobs strangled the words, and she fell silent.

Tovyah pulled away from her, rested his cheek against her, and smiled. If she didn't know better, she'd think he was giving her his permission to do what must be done.

"Oh, my sweet boy." She raised him to her shoulder and rubbed his back.

Miriam wandered into the room from the roof. She glanced at the basket, a soft blue blanket covering the bottom, then at Tovyah in her arms. Eyes wide, she turned to Kebi. "Are you doing it today?"

Her heart sank. She had hoped to spare Miriam from this. "I have to. He will surely be found soon."

"Can I go with you?" Her eyes glistened with unshed tears.

How did she deny her daughter these last moments with her baby brother? "All right. You can carry the basket. Get Aaron. We'll take him to Shiphrah's."

Kebi wrapped the cloth, attaching Tov to herself one last time, while Miriam ran to awaken Aaron. She ran back down the steps, little Aaron following more slowly, rubbing sleep from his eyes. She grabbed the bottom of the door and held it above her head. She looked right, then left, searching for Medjay.

Miriam grabbed the basket and Kebi followed her out the door, and they walked along the well-trod path to the river. Miriam stopped at the midwife's house, leaving Aaron there, then caught back up to Kebi.

Within strides of the water, Kebi halted and faced Miriam. "Say goodbye to him now, *motek*. I'm going on alone from here."

Miriam's little face twisted into a frown, tears rolling down her cheeks. "Yes, Imma." She set the basket down, kicking up a plume of dust. "May I first hold him?"

Kebi nodded and knelt.

Miriam's nimble fingers worked the knot on Kebi's wrap until the babe was free. She placed her hands on either side of his torso and lifted Tov to her shoulder.

His head on her shoulder, her arms securely around him, Miriam kissed his cheek. "Goodbye, my brother." Her little body shook as she sobbed. "I will miss you, motek."

Motek. *Sweetheart.* Miriam was never much for sentiment. She was practical, thoughtful. But apparently today called for a greater show of affection.

Kebi's heart thumped against her ribs, her stomach somersaulted. She squeezed her eyes shut. How much more could she take? *El Shaddai, give me strength.*

"You can take him, Imma," her daughter whispered. "Shall I wait here for you?"

"No, you go on. Go home. Find someone to play with." She cupped her cheek. "And dry your eyes before anyone sees you."

"Yes, Imma." Her words sounded strangled.

Tovyah in one arm, the basket in the other, Kebi stood and forced her feet to take the last few steps toward the river. It would be easier to throw herself into the Nile than to place her son in his basket.

She looked downstream to the washer women, her vision blurred by hot tears. Would one of them love her son as much as her own? Adoption was common in Egypt. Couples who had no children typically adopted a child. She searched for the woman she'd seen with no children, or at least no small ones that came to wash with her. If she'd wanted a child, why hadn't she adopted one already? Perhaps she didn't want any. Perhaps she was not yet married.

Perhaps El Shaddai was saving her for Tovyah.

His body would mark him as a Hebrew baby. Would they dare keep him? Any more than she did? If he were raised as an Egyptian, he certainly would never grow up to overthrow them, would he? He couldn't be the child of the prophecy. Wouldn't they see that? Wouldn't he be safe then?

Surely, even if none of those women would claim Tovyah, they would take him to someone who did. What kind of woman would just allow an innocent baby to remain in the floating basket in the river, with all the dangers it held?

What kind of woman would put him there?

Questions and doubts piled atop one another. If she didn't do it now, she never would.

She waded into a large group of bulrushes, fighting her way through until she was almost out again. She placed the basket on the water, allowing it to bounce against her shins. The water had risen just enough to allow the basket to float easily, yet not too quickly, even along the banks.

Kebi held him close, breathing in the sweet scent only babies shared. She kissed him, her lips lingering on his cheek. After a long moment, she wrenched his body away from hers. Her hands shaking, she laid him on the soft cloth in the bottom of the basket. Another went on top of him. She tucked it around him, wishing she never had to let go.

The crocodiles remained asleep on the sandbar. With a tiny shove toward the Egyptian mothers, Kebi set the basket free from the tangle of reeds. She watched as it drifted with the northward flow of the river, sailing farther away with every heartbeat.

She trudged back onto dry land. Ordering herself not to look back, she doubled over with paralyzing grief, sorrow and loss threatening to break her body in two. Crippling agony seized every muscle.

A few more steps. Against her better judgment, she looked over her shoulder. Her world narrowed to only the tiny basket bobbing on the waters of the Nile.

She startled as a gut-wrenching sound pierced the air. Had a crocodile claimed some oblivious gazelle as prey? Was a hippo in pain? She scanned the empty banks.

Horror grew as she realized the truth.

The sound had come from her.

CHAPTER FIVE

Then Pharaoh's daughter went down to the Nile to bathe, and her attendants were walking along the riverbank. She saw the basket among the reeds and sent her female slave to get it. She opened it and saw the baby. He was crying, and she felt sorry for him. "This is one of the Hebrew babies," she said.
~ Exodus 2:5–6 (NIV) ~

Kebi's feet felt as heavy as those on one of the king's colossal limestone statues. Shoulders slumped, she put one foot ahead of the other, battling the all-consuming urge to race back to the river, plunge into the water, and drag the basket to shore.

And never let Tovyah out of her sight again, as long as he lived.

Which wouldn't be for long with zealous, armed Medjay tramping around the villages searching for traitorous babes.

What kind of king fears an infant, anyway?

No, no matter how she looked at it, this was the only possible solution. The only way with a glimmer of hope for success.

She dabbed her eyes with her headcloth as she neared the village wall. There were spies everywhere, and how would she explain such sorrow from a simple trip to the river? She groaned, remembering that she'd meant to grab some rushes or flax before returning so it at least appeared she'd had a reason to go there. But the surprising force of her grief had left no room for such practical thoughts. Sucking in a long, slow breath, Kebi quickened her step.

As soon as she reached home, she slipped behind the reed door before Elli could stop her. Yanking on one end of her scarf, she headed for the back of the house. Talking to that vindictive woman was the last thing she needed this morning.

She kicked off her sandals, dropped to the ground, and reached for a piece of yesterday's flatbread. Leaning against the back wall, she ripped off a chunk and stuffed it in her mouth. It was tasteless, and if her body didn't need food whether she wanted it or not, she'd spit it out.

Shoving the last bite in her mouth, she leaned toward the grain jar and retrieved a scoop. There wasn't much left. She'd have to try hard to make it last until the next allotment.

The kernels pinged against the stone as she poured them onto the quern. She picked up the hand-stone and placed it on top of the golden grain. She willed herself to ignore the memory of helpless Tovyah drifting downstream as she leaned in and pushed the stone forward, then back. The thought of him in another woman's arms, at another's breast…

She shook her head as if she could set the captivating thoughts free.

The crunch of stone against barley began to soothe her. The kernels crushed under the weight and motion of the stone, crumbling into flour that would feed her family.

What was left of it.

The sand-colored grain at last turned into powder, she pushed it toward the center of the bottom stone, mounding a small pile of flour. She dipped the tips of her fingers in the center and swirled outward until she had a shallow depression in the center and poured leavening into the void. Then she added water, a little at a time, drawing it into the barley bit by bit until she had formed a soft dough.

Up on her knees, she began kneading the dough. Throwing her weight into her arms, she pulled and pushed and folded, then formed the dough into a round loaf. She dropped a square of cloth over it and left it to rise.

She rubbed her hands together, flicking away the last vestiges of sticky dough as she stepped into the sunlight of the central room.

It was exactly as she had left it earlier. And yet completely different.

Emptier. Hollow.

The pile of papyrus waited against the wall where she had left it. Infant-sized blankets lay neatly folded on the shelf along with their extra tunics.

Her throat constricted, a burn creeping up into her mouth as tears threatened to flow. She concentrated on Miriam, Aaron, and Amram. She still had a family, and they still needed her to care for them.

She grabbed the twig broom leaning against the wall and swept the clean floor. She was halfway done when Miriam burst inside.

"Imma! Imma!" Her round face was brightened by a smile that reached from ear to ear.

"Miriam, please don't yell. My head hurts already."

"But Imma, you'll never guess what happened!"

"What, motek?"

"I followed the basket and—"

Kebi gasped. She dropped the broom and rushed to her daughter, kneeling before her. She grasped her upper arms. "Miriam, do you realize how dangerous that was? I told you to go home." What if she had lost Miriam as well? The thought was too horrifying to even consider.

"But Imma, I saw her find the basket."

Hope flooded her soul. "One of the washerwomen?"

"Even better."

Better? What could be better than a mother finding him?

"It was the princess! The princess found him! She picked him up and held him and kissed him. Tovyah will be a prince!" Miriam all but danced, clapping her hands.

Kebi's heart stopped for a moment. The princess? Daughter of King Akhenaten, sister of King Tut? She hadn't been heard from since the ruling family left the new capital two years ago to return to Waset. No one knew whether she was even still alive or if she had been sacrificed in the violent turnover from Akhenaten to Tutankhamun.

Kebi rose and stepped away. The princess apparently had lived, but Tovyah would never be safe in the palace. He would be discovered as an Israelite and tossed into the Nile like so much refuse.

All her planning—hiding him for weeks, crafting a watertight basket, searching out the perfect mother for him—it had all been for nothing. How could this have gone so wrong?

Instead of saving Tovyah from the boy-king who wanted him dead, Kebi had placed him at his feet, an offering to his absurd fears.

Kebi swallowed her shock. "The princess? She'll just take him straight to her brother."

"No, Imma. She won't. She loves him. I could tell."

"How can you be so sure?"

Miriam shifted her weight, stared at her feet.

"Miriam?"

She raised her head, her little face scrunched into a wince. "I talked to her."

"You did what?" Kebi clenched her fists as if she could crumple her anger. She hadn't meant to raise her voice. "Start at the beginning. How do you know she is the princess? Maybe she is just an Egyptian with lots of land and fine clothes." Miriam had never seen the king, let alone the princess, so maybe this was just a terrible mistake. *Please, Shaddai.*

"When you left, I saw a group of people to the north coming toward the water. So I crept along the bank and hid in the reeds so I could see. One person was in a chair on poles carried on the shoulders of four men. They brought her to the edge of the water and set the chair down. The men went ahead of her, and they had clubs in their hands, I think to beat away any crocodiles. Maybe they don't know the crocodiles sleep in the middle of the river during the day and only the small ones that don't bite play by the edge. Maybe I should tell her if I see her ag—"

"Miriam! Please continue." Kebi stood and paced, biting the inside of her lip.

"The one in the chair stood up and waded into the water, and all the women stood on the bank watching her. She even had someone help her undress and wash." Miriam giggled.

That certainly sounded like a princess. Or at least someone very important from the palace.

Miriam's face sobered again. "Then she pointed at the reeds and told one of the others—I think she called her Neferet—to go see what it was." Her hands moved rapidly as she acted out the scene. "One of the men went with her, and Neferet waded over, pushed the bulrushes aside, and saw the basket. She called back to the princess, who told her to bring it. So she did, and when the princess took off the lid, she reached into the basket and pulled him out."

"Was he crying?"

"No! He seemed perfectly happy. She kissed him and held him—she loves him, I know." Miriam's wide eyes held nothing but complete confidence in her perception of the event.

Kebi felt woozy. *She* should be the one kissing his cheeks, not this...this *Egyptian*.

"Imma? Are you all right?"

She nodded. "Anything else?"

"She unwrapped him and checked him out all over—his fingers, his feet—"

Just as Kebi did after she birthed him.

"Then when she lifted his little tunic, she said, 'This is one of the Hebrew babies.' And then they all started talking at once, and most of them were saying she should throw him in the river. But she refused. She said her god had sent her this child."

More like my God. The living *God.*

"That's when I went over to her."

Kebi's heart nearly stopped. "*You* went to *her*? Miriam, how foolish you were!"

"No, she was very kind. I asked her if she wanted me to find a Hebrew wet nurse for the baby. She thanked me but said it would be easier to have someone at the palace do it, and she was sure she could find someone."

One moment's hope, shattered like pottery slammed on the ground.

Miriam frowned. "I'm sorry, Imma. I tried."

"Oh, Miriam. It's not your fault at all. I'm glad you wanted to make sure he would be safe. You are a very good sister."

Her smile returned.

And I am a very bad mother.

❖

It had been three days since Kebi placed Tovyah in the Nile. Three sunsets since she had held him, suckled him. Three sunrises since Miriam told her of the Egyptian woman kissing him.

Kebi's breasts were overfull, and the ache was more than physical. She wrapped a wide strip of coarse linen around her bust, as tightly as she could. The compression would help to dry up the milk.

As she ripped silvery sage leaves from the stem, she tried to divert her thoughts to something, anything other than her son. She dropped a handful of leaves into a pottery cup and poured hot water over it, then added a bit of honey to reduce the bitterness of the sage.

She'd downed enough in the last three days to float the king's barque. Why wasn't it working?

Or maybe it was. She vaguely remembered similar pain when she had to stop after Benjamin. With Miriam and Aaron it was so much easier. Their feedings gradually grew to be less often and further apart, until they were only once or twice a day by the time she weaned her child.

Not eight or nine.

She sat on an overturned pottery bucket by the firepit and sipped the sour brew.

The reed curtain rustled, but she didn't look up.

"Imma!" Miriam's shrill voice caused her to cringe.

Miriam rushed to her and halted, out of breath. "I was at the river, and I saw the woman who was with the princess the other day. Neferet? She said the princess had been looking for me."

Kebi's breath caught. What did a princess want with her daughter? She already had Kebi's son.

"She said the princess now wants a Hebrew nurse for Tovyah, and she asked if I could bring her one."

"She…she wants what?" Miriam must have heard wrong.

"She wants a Hebrew nurse for Tovyah. I told her I would bring one. I thought you would want to do it."

Kebi stared at Miriam, trying to decide whether she had actually heard what she had heard.

She could have Tovyah back? Or... "Do I have to live in the palace?"

Miriam's wide smile brightened even more. "No. She said you can keep him here until he is weaned."

Could El Shaddai really be giving her back her son? She sipped her tea—the tea she would no longer need if Miriam had gotten the story straight.

"Do you want to go?"

Kebi nearly spit out her drink. "Now?"

"Of course. She's waiting." Miriam had obviously inherited her gift of understatement from her father.

Kebi stood, glanced at her clothing. "I should put on a fresh tunic."

"Imma, you look fine. We need to go, or she'll find someone else." Miriam grabbed her hand and pulled her toward the door.

Kebi followed but stopped short. "What about Aaron?"

"He's with Nathanael. His imma will watch over him. I already asked her." When did Miriam become so sure of herself? So sure of everything?

Kebi followed Miriam to the western end of their street on the edge of the village. Just beyond the gates waited a gleaming chariot, covered with gold. Two six-spoke wheels were connected by a platform made of woven leather and surrounded by a waist-high guardrail on three sides.

A perfectly matched pair of cinnamon-colored horses were yoked to the vehicle, their heads towering above Kebi. Beaded blankets, clasped at the neck, covered their backs. One stamped a foot, sending dust into the air. The other stared at her with one eye, watching her every move. The closer she drew, the larger the animals seemed.

A young Egyptian woman beamed. Most Egyptians were taller than Israelites, but Neferet was about Kebi's height, slender, her immaculate, bleached white tunic draped perfectly on her body. "I am Neferet. Princess Beketaten has sent me to bring you to the palace. She will be so pleased. Join me." She gestured to the platform, where a wiry driver waited, the reins held loosely in his hands, wearing only a shenti and a dagger.

Kebi's eyes ran over the chariot, the horses, the driver. Her heart beat wildly. Neferet pointed to a small step hung off the back end of the platform. "Please."

Miriam hopped onto the step and then the floor, then turned to wait, her eyes asking why Kebi was taking so long to join her.

Kebi gathered her courage and placed one sandaled foot on the step, then the other onto the chariot.

Neferet stood behind her, a hand grasping either side of the guardrail, keeping them from falling out.

Or maybe preventing their escape. It was hard to tell. Who knew if the Egyptians told Miriam a wild story just to entice them to the palace?

But why would they want them, specifically? If they wanted more servants, all they had to do was take them. They'd done it often enough before.

The driver flicked the reins, and the horses began walking. When they reached the raised main road, far to the west beyond the area that would soon be flooded, he turned north, flicked again, and they began to run.

The ride was remarkably smooth. The soft floor absorbed much of the roughness of the road, allowing them to enjoy the view. A grin like Kebi had never seen before told her Miriam was thoroughly enjoying it.

The desert around them was beautiful in its own way. It wasn't the green land that sustained flocks of thousands of sheep, where Abraham, Isaac, and Jacob had lived, the land every Israelite dreamed of, waited for. But it had a stark, almost dangerous beauty, with hills made of golden sand and mysterious animals prowling at night.

Neferet tapped her on the shoulder and pointed ahead. "We're almost there." She smiled.

Kebi looked in the direction she pointed.

The palace of Tutankhamun rose in the distance like a ship sailing on a sea of sand. Walls painted a brilliant white, extending east toward the Nile, reached for the clouds.

They rounded a corner where the wall turned east before continuing north again. A wide gate occupied the middle of this new section, and the chariot slowed as they approached. Before them, slaves pulled open the wide double doors, and the driver steered the horses inside.

Kebi cringed as they neared the opening.

Had her unchecked desire to see her son again drawn them into danger?

CHAPTER SIX

❖

Pharaoh's daughter said to her, "Take this baby and nurse him for me, and I will pay you." So the woman took the baby and nursed him.
~ Exodus 2:9 (NIV) ~

Enormous stark-white pillars flanked the gates of the palace of the king. The horses trotted through the doors held open by Medjay armed with both bow and blade, their sour faces proclaiming they would, without hesitation, kill anyone who dared to intrude.

The driver steered the chariot to the right, then drew the horses to a stop at a smaller inner gate.

Neferet stepped off the platform then extended a hand to help Kebi while Miriam, face still bright as the light from an oil lamp, jumped down. They were led through the door and down a long hallway, brightly colored columns rising far above them on either side. Intricate patterns decorated the walls in a deep blue and gold. Plants in golden pots boasted huge green leaves.

The work it must take to keep the plants so large and green. Kebi could barely spare time enough to keep a few herbs alive. Some sage, mint.

The hallway ended in a large room open to the sky at the far end. Pedestals topped with sculptures randomly dotted the

A Mother's Sacrifice: Jochebed's Story

space. Vivid murals adorned the walls, depicting the king hunting or subduing his enemies. The floor was painted with scenes of a marsh filled with waterbirds and ducks, and hunters waiting to deploy an arrow. A water clock dribbled water from one jug into another.

Medjay lined the walls, spaced five or six strides apart. Long bronze spears clutched in their hands pointed straight and tall.

Kebi's knees were shaking as she waited for the princess to appear. She closed her eyes and offered up a silent plea to Shaddai. If her heart didn't slow down, she might faint.

From a single wide door in the far wall, the princess entered the room, four young Egyptian women behind her. Though Kebi had lived but a few years more, the princess looked decades younger. Her skin was flawless, her dark eyes outlined in green and blue. Lips stained a deep berry color accented cheeks that carried just the right amount of pink.

She was perfect.

Acutely aware of her weathered face, Kebi knelt, casting her gaze to the floor. Would the royal daughter consider her too old to nurse her new son?

She approached, her jeweled sandals barely making noise as she crossed the floor. "Rise."

Kebi obeyed.

The princess stood before her, a head taller. "I am Beketaten. This young girl found me and offered to find a Hebrew nursemaid for my son. I assume you are she?" Her eyes traveled from Kebi's head to her dusty feet.

Her cheeks heated under the princess's perusal. "I am."

"You appear healthy. You have no illnesses, nothing that would prevent you from performing your duty?"

"No, Princess."

"You are not nursing a child of your own?"

A Medjay spear could not have pierced her heart any more accurately. "I am not."

"And yet you are producing milk?"

"My son was…taken by the king's edict."

Beketaten's face paled. "And you are willing to nurture my son in his place?" Her voice had softened considerably.

"I am."

"I will double your grain allowance while you are nursing my son."

My son. Did she have to keep saying that? "Thank you. That is most generous of you."

"Not generous. I need you healthy in order to feed my son."

"Nevertheless." Kebi dipped her head.

"You will bring him to me once each week. My servant will come for you in the morning and return you to your village before the sun sets."

"Yes, Princess."

From the same door a young girl entered the room— holding Tovyah. It took every morsel of strength Kebi could summon to keep her attention on the royal daughter instead of her child.

"You are now responsible for a *sa nesut*, a prince. If anything happens to him, you and your family will suffer. If you have lied to me, I will know it. If he falls ill, I will know it. If he comes to any harm, I will know it. You will do everything in your power to keep him safe. He must come before any other responsibility, before your husband, before your other children. Nothing must interfere, do you understand?"

"I do."

She paused. "Do you have any others besides this little one?"

"This is my daughter, Miriam." She placed her hand on Miriam's shoulder. "And I have a son. This is his fourth summer." Aaron's sweet smile flitted through her mind.

"Very good. Do you have any questions?"

She avoided looking at the Medjay surrounding them. "The guards come to the villages every few days, searching for newborn males. What do I tell them?"

"Tell them this is the son of Beketaten, daughter of Akhenaten, sister of Tutankhamun." She shrugged, as if this were a foolish question.

"And what if they refuse to believe me?"

Beketaten frowned. "He is my son. You simply tell them that. Why would they not believe you?"

Neferet leaned near and whispered in the princess's ear.

Apparently just realizing the guards would have no reason whatsoever to believe Kebi—or any Hebrew about anything—Beketaten's mouth formed an *O*. "One moment." She whispered a reply to her maid, and Neferet hurried toward the door from which they had come.

"I will give you two amulets. Both have the cartouche of my name engraved on the pendant. You will wear one. Tie the other around the wrist of my son. If the Medjay give you any trouble whatsoever, show them the pendant."

Neferet returned, gold chains clutched in her fist. She opened her hand, and Beketaten picked up one of the necklaces.

"Here." Stepping closer, she allowed Kebi to see it before returning it to Neferet, who moved to stand behind Kebi, reaching around her and laying the pendant against her chest. Neferet's nimble fingers moved behind Kebi's neck, and then she returned to her place at Beketaten's side.

Kebi's hand went to her neck. She felt the smooth gold links and followed them down to the pendant. As long as her thumb, the oblong disk was covered in etching. She bowed her head. "Thank you, Princess."

The girl who held Tovyah placed the babe in the royal daughter's arms. The love on her face was agonizingly reassuring. Miriam was right. Her son would one day be raised by a caring mother.

But not by her.

◆

Kebi's heart pounded as the princess drew nearer, Tovyah cradled in her arms.

Beketaten paused a moment, staring at him. "Goodbye, my son," she whispered as she placed him in Kebi's arms. Tears gathered on her lashes.

Was it possible that this woman could truly love him? After only three days? Had El Shaddai arranged for the basket to float straight to someone who would protect him as eagerly as Kebi would?

As Beketaten slid her arms from under Tovyah, Kebi looked away. If she wasn't careful, tears would fall from her eyes as well, and what would the royal daughter have to say about that? Would she allow such a fierce competitor for the heart of a prince to get anywhere near him?

Doubtful.

Kebi held him close to her chest, resisting the urge to soak in his scent, to smother him with kisses. Milk suddenly threatened to rush from her body, leaving no doubt the babe was hers to anyone who saw her wet tunic.

Beketaten and her handmaidens hovered. As long as they stayed, Kebi wouldn't be able to rejoice in her son's return. She would have to remain poised, detached, as only his hired nurse while every part of her cried out to be his imma.

Beketaten turned to go.

Dare she call her back? "Princess?" She called so softly she wondered if the princess would hear her.

"Yes?" Beketaten paused and turned.

Kebi winced. She brought her free hand to her chest, heat rising from her chest to her cheeks. "I lost my son three days ago, and my milk… I need… Is there somewhere I could feed your son before the long walk back to the village?"

One perfect brow furrowed over moist eyes before understanding dawned. "Of course. Neferet will show you to a room. Then my chariot will take you home."

Kebi bowed, clutching Tovyah close. "Thank you."

"And if you ever use my name, please say Beket, not Beketaten. Especially if there are any court officials around."

"Yes, Princess."

Neferet tipped her head to the left. "This way, please."

Kebi placed a hand on Miriam's back. "Follow her, motek."

The pair followed the young girl to an empty room. A pair of long backless couches covered with brightly colored cushions stood along opposite walls. Miriam closed the door after Neferet left them alone.

The tears Kebi had held in escaped, chasing each other in rivulets down her cheeks and onto her neck. She kissed his face, counted fingers and toes again.

Tov snuggled his face into her tunic, whimpering.

"I think you missed me as much as I missed you." With one leg she pushed the couch flush against the wall and sat. Tovyah impatiently kicked his tiny feet, as he always did when he was hungry. Her fingers trembled as she struggled to untie her tunic at the neck. Her breast finally free, she positioned his head, and he latched on instantly, as if no time at all had lapsed since she last fed him. The pain in her left breast eased as Tov suckled greedily.

She inspected the fine tunic he was dressed in. She'd put him in the best one she had before she placed him in the Nile. What had happened to it? Obviously they didn't think it appropriate for a prince.

When milk began to leak from her right breast, she hurriedly switched sides. As the ache receded, Kebi leaned against

A Mother's Sacrifice: Jochebed's Story

the wall, nourishment flowing from her body to his. The way it was meant to be. The way it should be, always.

Thank You.

El Shaddai had given him back to her. For a time, at least.

◆

Kebi jumped as the door was shoved open. She'd heard no knocking. Glancing at Miriam, she realized her daughter had had no notice either. Miriam scrambled to her feet and ran to Kebi's side.

An older Egyptian woman entered. Her nearly sheer, exquisitely pleated linen tunic and jeweled sandals denoted a high status. This was no servant.

"I am Maia. I am the *menat nesut.*"

The royal nurse?

"I nursed Tutankhamun Hekaiunushema, Beautiful of Laws Who Quells the Two Lands, Who Makes Content All the gods. I was also the nurse of his sister, Beketamun."

Didn't she say her name was Beketaten?

"I am now the Great Royal Nurse, leader of all the *menatu*. You will answer to me. You will obey me precisely. Am I clear?" Her cracking voice belied the authority she clearly owned.

Too afraid to speak, Kebi nodded.

"You will address me as Maia. You will address the princess as *nebet-i.*"

"Yes, Maia." *Nebet-i*. She thought quickly through her Egyptian vocabulary. *My lady.*

Unlike most of the royal Egyptian women she'd seen, this one wore no intricately styled wig. Short, graying hair set off her round face untouched by any makeup. A wide necklace, made of four rows of golden disc beads, graced her neck.

"Tell me. Do you have children of your own?"

Kebi patiently answered the same questions Beketaten had already asked her.

Maia aimed a glare her way. "You should know I was against the hiring of you."

What had she done to incur this woman's wrath? Kebi stammered. "I'm sor—"

She waved a hand. "Not you, particularly. Any Israelite. But the prince would not allow anyone to suckle him. Beket thought perhaps an Israelite mother nursed her children in a different way or did something he was used to that we had no knowledge of." She stared at Kebi as she nursed Tovyah. "I don't find that to be true."

How was she supposed to answer that?

"There are many regulations you must now observe. Everything you do will affect your ability to nourish the sa nesut. By nursing him you become related. This milk relationship is nearly as strong as one formed by blood. Your children are now milk-siblings, and their behavior must be beyond reproach." She turned her hard gaze on Miriam, who scooted back on the bench and hid her face between Kebi and the wall.

Kebi twisted to wrap a protective arm around her.

"You will not become pregnant. There can be no competition for your attention or your milk."

What would Amram say about this? He didn't even know she'd come to the palace. She couldn't possibly ignore her other children and give all her attention to Tov. They needed her too.

But she would have them for the rest of their lives, while she would have Tov for only a couple of years.

"As Beket has said, you are to present him here every week. Beket will spend the day with him."

"Yes, Maia."

"Her chariot will appear in your village just after dawn. You will be returned home before dark. As I said, I don't want you here. I do not think you are a suitable menat for a prince. I will see if you are properly caring for the child, and I will know if you have neglected your duty in any way." She held up one bony finger. "One mistake, and you will be sent away, without any wages and only after being properly punished."

"Yes, Maia."

"One week, then." She turned to go, but at the door she stopped. "That's ten days, not seven. A true week, an Egyptian week." She threw open the door and strutted out.

Kebi let out a long sigh. She didn't belong here, most emphatically wasn't wanted here. Every part of her was disparaged, deemed inferior.

Yet they must know Tovyah was Hebrew, not Egyptian. Did all of them know? Or only Beket and Maia, maybe also the women with her?

Did the king know?

Though his body would remain Israelite, when they were through with him, would he ever admit his true heritage? After he'd been taught to worship the false gods of Egypt, to revere the boy-king as a god, to despise the people who had given him life?

How could he deliver Israel from their hated captors if he was one of them?

CHAPTER SEVEN

❖

*Children are a heritage from the L*ORD*, offspring a reward from him.*
~ Psalm 127:3 (NIV) ~

Kebi sat in the evening shade of the side room nursing Tovyah. The stifling heat of summer seemed not to have lessened at all, and even though the sun was nearly behind the mountains to the west, sweat dripped down her back. Maia's harsh words had been forgotten, for the moment. Kebi's dry mouth demanded water, but she dare not move. Not yet.

Quenching her thirst could wait. The cool of night could wait. Everything could wait until Tovyah was satisfied and happy.

Amram stepped through the door and bent to place his sandals in the basket. He moved from the shade into the courtyard, and his eyes widened. "What is he doing here?" He glanced at the reed door, which Kebi had tied open to allow fresh air. He jerked on the end of the rope and let the curtain tumble closed. "Why isn't he with the princess?" His eyes darted from her, to his son, to the door, and back. He shook his head. "What did you do? Please tell me you didn't somehow take him back."

Her mouth fell open. "You think I sneaked into the palace of the most powerful man in the world, located the princess's rooms, found Tovyah, and sneaked back out, all without being heard or seen?" How could he think that of her?

Then again, she had done a great many things in the last three months neither she nor Amram would ever have imagined.

"I have no idea what you did! Explain it to me." Though he didn't say it aloud, his eyes pleaded with her to return him so the king's Medjay wouldn't be storming into his house at any moment to drive a dagger through his heart.

"The princess wanted a Hebrew nursemaid. Apparently he wasn't allowing anyone else to suckle him, and she thought it was because we were somehow different." She smiled down at Tovyah, his cheek resting on her breast, full and sleepy. "I think he just wanted me. Anyway, she hired me to be his nurse until he is weaned."

"She just gave him up, just like that?" His tone was just short of mocking.

Beket's despondent features hovered in the back of Kebi's mind, though she'd tried desperately to forget. "I have to take him back once each Egyptian week for her to see him. I think she was actually quite reluctant to let him go."

"She was? What makes you say that?" His panic abated for now, he sat beside her, long legs crossed at the ankles.

"She was about to cry, as if she was giving up her own son. I think she truly cares for him." She paused. "*She*, however, is assured he will not be eaten by crocodiles." Kebi tried unsuccessfully to keep the bitterness from her voice.

Amram leaned his head against the wall. "I'm sure the edict is not her doing."

Kebi shrugged, unwilling to give the princess any credit.

"Can I hold him?" Amram's voice was a whisper.

"Of course. He's your son."

He stretched out his arms, and she placed the sleeping babe into them. The smile on his face was a just reward for the pain of the last three days.

Joy bloomed within her. Tovyah was where he belonged.

◆

Kebi found herself humming early the next morning as she broke several loaves of barley bread into a large, wide-mouthed jug of water and stirred to break up the pieces even further. She draped a piece of cloth over the jug and left it to ferment.

She removed the cloth from the jug beside it and picked it up. Placing a sieve over a third jar, she poured the contents of the second jar into the third. Chunks of bread remained on the cloth and the filtered beer streamed out.

The drink was not particularly tasty, at least to her. She added honey, when available, to sweeten the bitter brew a bit. But the fermentation process made the Nile's questionable water safe to drink. And it was nothing like the strong beer the Egyptians used to celebrate with, leaving them free of inhibition and good judgment.

Amram came down the steps, and Kebi handed him a cup of beer and a slice of leftover flatbread. Amram downed the drink, kissed her cheek and Tovyah's head, and left to serve the Egyptians.

Since the first jug was empty, more water was needed. Kebi stepped out of her home and nearly ran into Shiphrah.

"Oh! I'm sorry!" The midwife stepped back. Her eyes rested on the tiny bundle resting against her. "I see the rumors are true."

Kebi couldn't stop the smile that took over her face. "It is. He has been returned to us. For a while."

Shiphrah's smile faded. "Let's go back inside."

"Why? I was going to the river for water."

"Send Miriam."

Fear creeping up her neck, she stepped back inside. "Miriam? Please take your brother and fetch the water."

"Yes, Imma." Miriam grasped Aaron's hand, then retrieved the water jar from Kebi before leaving.

When the door bounced closed, she looked to Shiphrah. "What is it? Why such secrecy?"

"It's not really secrecy. I just thought I should tell you that not everyone is as thrilled with your new arrangement as you are."

"What do you mean? Why not?"

"Why not? Because many mothers have lost their sons, and now you miraculously have yours back."

How was that her fault? "That wasn't my intention! I was trying to give him away."

"Even then, your son would have been alive, when so many others have died."

"Are you saying I shouldn't have done what I did?" She scoffed. "It's not my fault no one else thought of it."

"Of course not. And I don't think that's what most of them think. But there are a couple who are quite angry."

"At me? What did I do?"

"I don't think they're really angry at you. They're angry at the king, or at Shaddai for not preventing it to begin with. But you will be the obvious target. I just wanted to warn you."

"What do I do now?"

"I don't know."

"Who do you mean by 'a couple'?"

Shiphrah winced. "I don't want to stir up any more trouble."

"Elisheba?"

Shiphrah nodded.

"Anyone else?"

Shiphrah closed her eyes. "No," she said softly.

Kebi's joy evaporated like smoke from a cooking fire. Elisheba and Joel exerted a great deal of influence in the village, especially since he had been named supervisor of the men of this village. They could turn many of the people here against them. Kebi was deemed inferior at the palace, Amram wasn't sure he could trust her judgment, and now the mothers of her own village blamed her for the loss of their sons.

"Kebi, it's not that bad. They'll get over it. But for a while at least, maybe don't parade him around the village. Give people a chance to get used to the fact that Shaddai has given you back your son but not theirs. They'll adjust, and I believe soon enough they will rejoice with you. Just give them some time for the sting to fade." She smiled and stretched out her hands. "Why don't you let me hold him while you help Miriam with the water?"

Kebi allowed Shiphrah to take Tovyah, then headed to the river.

The river gave life each year with its flood, and also took it. The village, with its tiny houses and common walls, gave them community and also allowed every action to be judged by others. Shaddai gave Tovyah back, but in the process Kebi might lose her friends, her support.

Why must everything be so double-edged?

◆

Kebi dressed in the dark. The sun wouldn't raise its head above the Nile for quite a while, but she dared not be late the first time she was supposed to present Tovyah at the palace.

She jumped as Amram touched her shoulder.

"Why did you awaken so early?"

"I don't want to be late. Maia said—"

"I remember what she said. But she also said *after* dawn."

Fear creeped along her spine. "I don't want to see anyone. I'll just go wait at the edge of the village."

He wrapped his arms around her from behind, his chin resting on her shoulder. "Anyone? Or Elisheba?" he asked.

Normally she loved his embrace, but today it irritated her. "Does it matter?" She wrenched away from him, still not facing him.

"I suppose not. But I don't think any of the others are angry that you still have your son. A little jealous maybe, but I think most are happy for us."

"You don't see the looks I get. They would stop a lion in its tracks."

He gently turned her to face him. "Looks from whom?"

Elisheba, mostly.

He took a step nearer. "They all know we don't get to keep him forever. In a few years, at most, we'll be just like they are."

Horrible, bloody images of ax-wielding Medjay clutching screaming baby boys flashed through her mind. "I believe any mother who had her son fed to the crocodiles would do just about anything for a few more days, a single hour with her child."

He drew her into his arms again. This time she didn't resist, and his strength flooded her. "El Shaddai will watch over you. Both of you." His warm breath caressed the back of her neck. Why couldn't she stay here in the village with her son forever? Pretend the king and his revolting orders didn't exist?

He pulled back and rested his hands at her waist.

She nodded toward the firepit. "I ground the flour for today. It's in the smaller jar by the barley pot."

His dimple appeared as one corner of his mouth turned up. "When did you do that?"

"Before you came down."

"In the dark?"

"I lit a lamp. I had to. Shiphrah doesn't have the time, and Miriam lacks the strength. She can make the bread, though."

"I assumed we'd have to do without." He bent to kiss her tenderly. "Thank you for thinking of us."

"I have to leave. Would you bring Tovyah down for me?"

"Of course."

Kebi chose a cloth from a basket in the corner and settled it on her head, throwing one end over her shoulder.

Amram reappeared, Tov's head on his shoulder. He placed a hand on Tov's back and allowed him to fall away from his chest, placing a soft kiss on his cheek. "Shalom." His whisper was barely audible.

She slipped out the door while she still had some courage left, trying to forget that every goodbye brought her one closer to the day she would return alone.

At the end of the village road, on the edge of the desert, the chariot waited. Kebi searched for Neferet. Only a tall, brawny man stood to the side, reins in his hand. He faced away from her, moving a large hand down the nose of one of the horses. He wore a pleated linen shenti with a loose shirt held by straps over his shoulders.

Kebi's steps slowed as she approached. Was she expected to ride in this chariot alone with this man, this stranger? Amram certainly would not approve.

She'd simply have to tell him to go to the palace and implore Neferet to return with him.

She cleared her throat.

He turned, his striped, chin-length headdress swinging with the motion. He was older than she'd first assumed, about the same age as her oldest brother—Amram's father—if she had to guess. A curved blade hung from his belt, reaching below his knees. Three golden bees suspended on a gold chain rested against his shirt. A rare symbol of valor in battle.

She froze. It was the same guard who had come into their home and left without looking under the stripped reeds. If he recognized her, he would know she'd been hiding Tovyah. He'd know how old the baby was. He could tell King Tutankhamun about them or just take his *kopesh* to them himself, right here, right now. Let her blood sink into the tawny sand as he carried little Tovyah to the river.

But he said nothing. His smile was soft, and his eyes were kind. Like her abba's had been.

Maybe he didn't want to kill Israelite babies for no reason. Maybe that's why he walked out of her house two weeks ago.

She stepped forward, and he held out a hand. She took it and tried to step onto the chariot's woven platform, but her feet became tangled in her dress. With one hand in his and one arm around Tovyah, she couldn't lift up her tunic. How would she ever get up there?

"May I hold him for you?" His gentle voice contradicted his obvious strength. He held out two muscular arms, palms up.

Should she hand over her infant Hebrew son to the Chief of the Medjay?

If she didn't, how would she get on the chariot and to the palace? If she didn't take Tovyah to the princess, what would be the repercussions?

He'd allowed Tovyah to live before, hadn't he?

She placed her son in his arms, and he cradled him to his broad chest.

After she stepped up, he handed Tovyah back, a sly grin on his face. "My name is Mahu."

"My name is Jochebed, but I am called Kebi."

"*Em hotep,* Kebi."

She forced a smile. "Shalom."

He flicked the reins, and they took off. "From now on, I will be the one picking you up each week and returning you home."

Surely someone in his position had better things to do than pick up a slave.

Was he being punished for some error? Or was he sent here to make sure she showed up, to take her by force if necessary?

Kind eyes or not, he was a Medjay. And the Medjay were sworn to protect Egypt with their lives.

Did he know she held in her arms a threat greater than the Mitanni, greater than the Hittites?

And what would he do if he found out?

CHAPTER EIGHT

Then a new king, to whom Joseph meant nothing,
came to power in Egypt.
~ Exodus 1:8 (NIV) ~

PAENIPAT, SECOND MONTH OF AKHET, THE SEASON OF INUNDATION

Kebi held tight to the guardrail of the chariot as Mahu made a hard right turn toward the eastern gate of the palace complex.

The guard steered the vehicle through the gate and veered right toward the door leading to the western palace. After he helped Kebi down, he stepped back up and belted a command at the animals. The sound of trotting horses fell away.

The inner door seemed much larger today. Last time, if she'd been sent away, she'd have been no worse off than when she arrived. But this time…if she was found wanting, not only would she lose Tovyah—a second time—she'd be whipped.

She didn't remember Medjay stationed on either side of the inner door either. A leather strap ran from one shoulder to the opposite hip. They stood feet apart, bow in hand, ax on the hip.

Eyes on her.

"I am here to see the princess." She swallowed. "I have her son." Her voice dropped to a whisper.

The guards continued staring at her. Should she just go in? Beket was expecting her. She raised one foot, but before she could set it down, they grasped the handles of their blades.

Now what? She couldn't let Beket think she had decided not to honor their agreement. It had been made quite clear that if she didn't, the consequences would be dire.

Heavy footfalls sounded behind her. She turned to see Mahu. He marched past her and stood before the men, who snapped their feet together and stood straight as pillars.

"Captain." They spoke in unison.

Captain? He was only a captain? With those bees around his neck?

"This woman"—Mahu turned to acknowledge her—"will be coming each week. You will allow her to enter the western palace without hindrance."

"Yes, Captain." The guard on the right turned to grasp the handle of the door, revealing the quiver full of arrows resting against his lower back, ends extending toward the waist for easy access. He pulled the door wide open, then gave her a brief nod.

Mahu turned toward her and smiled. "Enter." He extended a hand toward the palace.

Kebi preceded him though the doorway, then stepped aside to let him pass her. Once through the anteroom, they entered an expansive room surrounded by brightly colored pillars, open to the sky at the far end.

Beket was waiting, and she immediately moved toward them, her nearly sheer linen tunic hugging her body, revealing far too much in Kebi's opinion. How could she walk around like that in front of men who were not her husband?

Beket reached for Tovyah, and Kebi allowed her to take him, ignoring the searing ache in her heart.

"How is my beautiful son today?" Beket drew a finger down his cheek. "It seems you have grown in only one week." She glanced up at Kebi, barely registering her presence. "How was he this week? Sleep well? No problems?"

"He did beautifully. He sleeps peacefully, eats as he should. He is delightful."

"Of course he is delightful. He is a prince." Beket turned and headed for a grouping of wide, gilded chairs with legs ending in lion's paws and backs made of woven leather. She sat in one and settled Tovyah on her lap. "How could anyone give you away?"

Kebi closed her eyes, the anguish of that day overwhelming her. This princess had no idea what life was like for a slave.

Beside her, Mahu cleared his throat.

She opened her eyes to see him tip his head toward her.

Beket hurried near to place a hand on her arm. "I am so sorry. I know you had your children taken from you because of my brother. I just meant… I can't even imagine what it would be like."

No, you can't.

She beamed at Tovyah. "I have decided on his name. I drew him from the waters of the Nile because the Aten, giver of life, has blessed me with this child. Therefore he shall be called Aten-Mose, born of Aten."

The heat of shame crept up Kebi's neck to her cheeks, and she lowered her head to hide her face. To see her son's name changed from proclaiming the goodness of El Shaddai to one honoring a false god? She would rather Mahu slice her chest open with his kopesh, rip her heart out, and stomp on it.

"Do you need me any longer, Princess?" Mahu asked.

"No, thank you, Mahu. I do love seeing you. I miss you." She gave him a one-armed hug.

He kissed her temple. "You were always my favorite. But don't tell your brother."

Beket laughed. "And you were mine."

Grinning, the guard left the room.

Neferet appeared. "Come. I'll show you to Mose's rooms." She gestured to the doors on the right side of the hall.

Rooms? How many did a baby need, especially one who would visit once a week? The left—with only one door, from which Beket had entered last week—must be the princess's rooms. Smaller rooms, evidenced by eight or ten doors, spanned the length of the right wall. In the center, one door stood open.

Neferet looked over her shoulder. "This way."

Kebi followed her into a room much bigger than it had appeared from the outside. A raised bed stood against the north wall, a canopy of sheer linen draped over it. A row of small windows sat high in the far wall. An open door was next to a couch on the south wall. What was in there? And was that part of his space as well?

"This room is the brightest of all of them. The sun comes through the windows, but since it's from the south it doesn't overheat it." She moved to the bed. "He'll nap here while he's in the palace." Stuffed cushions lined the head of the bed, and several children's toys were sprinkled atop the bright blue fabric that covered it.

Tovyah's room alone was ten times bigger than their dirt-floor, mud-brick home. He would have everything he could imagine, and more than he could ever dream of.

How would she ever compete?

◆

The morning passed quickly, Beket asking question after question—about his care, his habits, his personality. Kebi fed Tovyah again and helped Beket put him down for his morning nap. While he slept, Kebi examined the carved wooden and ivory toys, showing Beket which he would enjoy now and which would need to be saved until he was older.

After a midday meal, with better food than Kebi had ever tasted, she sat cross-legged on the backless couch in Tovyah's room. She positioned him against her and helped him to find his place while she settled her mind.

A cat—what had Beket called her? Miu—padded through the room until she curled up under the couch. Kebi slid down the couch so her feet weren't next to the animal. She was still closer than Kebi would have liked, but at least Kebi wouldn't have to look at her if she stayed under there.

Beket had gone to the river to bathe, probably to the very spot where she had claimed Kebi's child as her own. Her attendants had followed, leaving all the rooms in the western palace empty. There was no Beket. No edict. No horrible king.

There was only Mose.

No, Tovyah. *Her* child.

That morning, Tovyah had awakened from his nap, crying. Not yet hungry, for she had fed him before he lay down. Beket had rushed to his side, tried to comfort him. The princess hadn't even cast a glance her way.

Kebi had known what to do to calm the babe, but instead she'd been forced to sit on the couch on the other side of the room and listen to her son, his distress clearly evident to all.

She shifted Tovyah to the other side and studied his face. How beautiful he was. Long lashes fluttered at her as he returned her interest. He reached toward her, and she brought her hand near. He gripped a finger with a chubby fist.

Beyond the nursery, the door to the main hall slammed against the wall as it burst open.

Tov pulled back, his face uncertain.

"Shhh." She forced her mouth into a wide smile. "We're fine. Everything is fine."

He returned to suckling.

Sandaled feet stomped in unison outside in the hall, the noise growing louder with each step. Shuddering, she realized they were headed for the nursery.

Kebi hurriedly threw her head cloth over her chest.

Miu scrambled under the bed as four muscled, broad-shouldered Medjay entered the room. With the door open, who was to stop them? They entered and scattered in four directions, searching, their eyes taking in everything. Apparently satisfied no hidden threats awaited, they parted and revealed King Tutankhamun in the doorway.

The ruler was not quite a teen, barely more than a child, his smooth face belying the absolute power he wielded. His knee-length linen tunic, loosely belted at the waist, was set off by a wide, jewel-studded collar that mirrored the neck of his garment. A simple gold band, a rearing cobra at the front, encircled his shaved head.

He quickly scanned the room, and finding Kebi alone, turned his hard gaze on her. "Where is your nebet?"

"Beketaten has gone to bathe. She should be back soon."

A half smile appeared, then disappeared just as quickly. He took three long strides toward the bed, perused the toys still scattered upon it. "Beketaten? Is that what she said her name was?"

Had she just landed Beket in trouble? Beket had asked her not to use her full name in front of any officials. "Yes." She dragged the word out.

"We shall see about that." He marched back to face her. "And who are you?"

"I am the baby's nurse."

"And what makes you think you are qualified to give sustenance to a royal son?"

I'm his mother.

She swallowed her pain. "I've nursed two children of my own. Both are healthy." She withered under his continued stare. "Umm, well, Beket thought—"

Laughter drifted in from the path to the river.

The king left the bedroom, followed by the guards.

Beket and her attendants swarmed into the central hall. At the sight of the king, the attendants dropped to a knee. Still holding Tovyah, Kebi joined them. Beket bowed from the waist.

"Leave us." The king waited until the women and his guards rose and left the room.

Kebi rose as well, but he held out a hand, palm facing her. "Wait."

Kebi's blood pounded in her ears. He obviously didn't approve of her. What would he do? Send her away?

The king stepped nearer to his sister, who was a head taller than he was. "I go on a hunting trip with my wife. I return to hear—not from you—that you have a son?"

She smiled and crossed to take Tovyah from Kebi, then presented him to the king. "This is your nephew, Aten-Mose. For Aten has given me the child I had not dared to wish for."

His face darkened. "First you refuse to change your name to Beket-Amun, and now you are audacious enough to call your son 'born of Aten'? Have you no respect at all for your king?"

Beket raised her chin. "Are you ordering me to change my name? Or his? If you are, and I mean *you*, not Vizier Ay, then of course I will obey. But if this is not a command, I will not abandon the god I was raised *by our father* to worship as the sole god of Egypt."

"Of course it is not my command." His voice softened. "But perhaps you can call him Mose? At least in my hearing. And that of the vizier."

"That I will gladly do. I have no desire to anger you or make things difficult for you."

He embraced her, his head against her shoulder. "You and Ankhesenamun are the only sisters I have left. My only family. And you are the only one who shares my blood completely."

Kebi breathed a sigh of relief as Beket bent to kiss the king's cheek, and he smiled.

Tovyah was once again safe.

For now.

❖

The day had been longer and more exhausting than Kebi expected. Having someone scrutinize every little movement made everything twice as hard. The ride to the village was mostly silent.

Mahu stepped off the chariot first, then extended a hand to Kebi. Half of the sun hid below the horizon, half was still visible.

"Thank you," she said.

He smiled and climbed back into the vehicle. "I'll wait until you reach the village."

"Thank you again."

She was just inside the gate when Elisheba marched toward her. "I saw you in that chariot. An Egyptian chariot. Where did you go?"

"I take the baby to the daughter of the king, as she has commanded."

"If it's her baby, why does he live with you?"

"She hired me as his wet nurse."

Elli cackled. "Why would she hire *you* when there are so many Egyptian women who would fight to do it for her? For no wages at all?"

Good question. Kebi thought fast. "She doesn't trust the others. She doesn't want someone who will grow attached to him and cause problems later. She wants someone who will never see him again after he is weaned." She ignored the sting of that thought.

Elli eyed her. "What did you give them to allow this arrangement? What about the driver? He seems quite protective of you. Maybe you are giving *him* something."

Kebi's cheeks flamed. "He is the princess's bodyguard. He is protective of her son, not me."

"I don't believe you." Elli grabbed at Tovyah. "This is *your* son, isn't it? That explains why we never saw the daughter you claim you had, but your son was never taken to the Nile either." She tried to wrest Tovyah from Kebi's arm, much as the Medjay had ripped her son from hers not that long ago. "Why should the princess choose your son to save and raise as her own? What was wrong with mine? Is yours special in some way? Let me see him."

"You're hurting me. Stop!" Kebi twisted away, protecting Tovyah with her body. Elli reached around her, grabbing at the wrap that held him to Kebi's chest.

"Leave her alone." Amram's voice startled them both as he strode toward them from the direction of the brickfields. One strong arm gently gripped Kebi's forearm, and with his other he plied Elli's away. "Why are you hurting my wife? And…the baby?"

Elli's face reddened, whether from embarrassment or anger was hard to tell. "She was grabbing me."

"Your hand was on her, not the other way around."

Elli fidgeted, her head down. "I… I…" She glanced up, and her face brightened momentarily. Then a fearful look came over her. "Joel. Help me, please."

Kebi looked over her shoulder to see Elisheba's husband marching quickly toward them, a scowl darkening his face and a coiled whip in his hand.

"What's happening here? Why are you all out here instead of in your homes? It's nearly dark."

Elli pointed a long finger at Kebi. "She was flaunting that child. When I begged her to stop, she grabbed at me and threw me away from her."

Kebi tried to calm the anger rising up within her. "That's not true!"

"It's not true. I saw it. Your wife was nearly crawling over Kebi, trying to get to the child."

"Joel, believe me. I did no such thing." A stray tear fell from Elli's eyes. She probably conjured it up just to convince her husband.

"You two, get back inside." He gestured toward the houses with his whip.

Amram stepped toward him and looked down on the shorter man. "You may be the foreman in the mud pits, but here you don't have the authority to order us to do anything."

Joel smirked. "Still, you should go. Before anything else happens." He opened his fingers and let the end of the whip fall to the ground.

Amram slipped a protective arm around Kebi and steered her toward home.

"Can he hurt you? In the fields?"

"I'm not under him. I'll be all right."

"Are you sure?"

He turned to her and smiled, though the smile didn't reach his eyes. "I'm sure."

That night, as she lay on the roof watching the long-tailed star on one of its last journeys, far to the south, something told her they hadn't heard the last from Joel.

CHAPTER NINE

✦

"Look," [the king] said to his people, "the Israelites have become far too numerous for us. Come, we must deal shrewdly with them or they will become even more numerous and, if war breaks out, will join our enemies, fight against us and leave the country."
~ Exodus 1:9–10 (NIV) ~

Kebi's second visit to the palace was going much like the first—caring for Tovyah while on display. When he lay down for his nap, she was at a loss as to how to occupy her time. At home there was always more to do than there was time for. Here, she was wasting large chunks of time. She'd try to remember to bring some mending from home next week.

In the main hall, under the open roof, she waited with Beket for the attendants to bring the midday meal. Kebi would have preferred to eat alone, perhaps in Tovyah's room, but Beket wanted her near in case she needed help with Tovyah. With *Mose*. She had no choice but to obey. Still, it was awkward.

"This time of year I have to make sure I eat before the sun is directly overhead or it's too hot here. Still, I just love seeing the sky. Nearly all the buildings in my father's city were open to the sky. Father said that was so we could see the Aten."

The attendants had just entered the hall, pitchers and platters in hand, when the front door swung open.

Tut marched in, flanked by four guards. He approached them, his gaze never wavering.

The handmaidens scurried away while Beket rose to greet him. "Is it really necessary for you to bring guards into my personal rooms? Do you really think me a threat?"

"It's not you I am worried about. I've brought my astrologer. He will examine the boy to make sure he is not one of the Hebrew babies who should have been destroyed."

Kebi's blood ran cold, but Beket's face remained calm. She stepped nearer to her brother. "You don't trust me?"

Tut leaned near, his face a hand's breadth away. "I don't trust anyone when it comes to my kingdom." He hissed like one of Egypt's hooded snakes. "Now, let us see the child."

Beket held Tovyah with his back against her, one hand under his bottom, the other on his chest.

Tut nodded to one of his guards standing by the door. The dark-skinned, muscled Medjay opened it, and an old, stooped man leaning on a walking stick hobbled in. He wore a deep indigo robe over an ankle-length tunic. Several long chains dangled from his neck, each with an amulet or charm. A young boy followed him, a bag hung across his chest, carrying several scrolls.

These men wielded almost as much power as the king. Some said more. Many believed that Beket and Tut's father, Akhenaten, had been murdered because he had decreed the Aten was the only god, depriving these star-watchers—not to

A Mother's Sacrifice: Jochebed's Story

mention the powerful priests of Amun—of the lucrative lifestyle they had enjoyed. A ruler more a child than a man was much more easily controlled.

Somehow watching the night sky imbued these men with great authority. They sat in small rooms on the edges of the palace grounds, studying the stars and following their paths across the night sky. They sat cross-legged on the floor and read and reread old scrolls.

They told the king a baby was his greatest enemy, and everyone believed it without question.

Gold bracelets on his wrinkled arms clinked as he neared baby Mose. He halted before the princess, studying the infant. "When was he born?"

"I was not there, so I don't know." Beket held his gaze. "And neither does anyone else."

I was there. I know.

The astrologer lifted one of Mose's feet with one finger. "He looks very much to me as though he was born under the sign of the long-tailed star." He turned to Tut. "Unless she can prove he wasn't, I would not take the risk."

Beket grabbed Mose's foot from him. "Maybe you should have to prove he was."

Tut stepped forward and looked up at her. "You forget who you are talking to. You are my sister, but this child may be a threat, not only to my kingdom but to all of Egypt. I cannot—will not—take the chance."

Kebi's heart pounded against her ribs. How could she have come this far, still to have him destroyed? She squeezed her eyes shut tightly. *El Shaddai, help me!* She took a tentative step forward.

Beket raised an eyebrow.

"May I say something?" Kebi's voice wavered.

Beket glared at her.

Tut ignored her.

The astrologer smirked.

A mere slave wouldn't dare speak without first being asked.

Kebi folded her hands together, clenching until her fingers turned pink. No one had yet told her to shut up, so she ventured on. "His front teeth have already appeared. This happens usually four months or more after the child has been born, so it would appear he was born *before* the long-tailed star appeared."

The old man narrowed his eyes at her before returning his attention to Mose. He raised a trembling hand, then slipped one crooked finger into Mose's mouth. He moved it back and forth over the lower gum.

Kebi backed away and concentrated on the design painted on the floor. Mose cooed.

The star-watcher removed his finger, the corners of his lips turned up. "The slave speaks the truth. His teeth have punctured the gum. Barely, but they're there."

Tut frowned. "Are you sure?"

The man straightened as far as he could, given the curve of his back. "I fathered seven children. Four lived to have children of their own. Of these, fifteen lived. None of them felt the pain of teeth ripping their way through the gums before four months old. Most, closer to six."

Tut narrowed his eyes. "Are you sure enough to risk the security of Egypt's future?"

"Yes." He tilted his head. "Are you?"

Tut placed his hand on Mose's head. His face softened. "Yes." He turned and marched from the room, his guards behind him.

The astrologer smiled. "What is his name?"

"Mose," Beket said.

"May the gods watch over him." He turned and shuffled toward the door.

Kebi blew out a long breath. *Thank you, El Shaddai.*

Beket turned to Kebi. "Why did you do that?" Her voice said she was more shocked than angry.

Kebi jerked her head up. What had she done? "Do what?"

"Tell the astrologer Mose must be more than three months old."

What should she say? "He is a prince. I didn't want any harm to come to him."

Beket studied her face. "It's more than that, I think."

"I saw far too many boys thrown to the crocodiles. If I can save one more, shouldn't I?" She gave Beket a weak smile, then accepted Mose from her.

Kebi laid Mose down on the elaborate bed that would sleep her entire family and lay down next to him. *El Shaddai, thank You for protecting Tovyah yet again. Thank You his teeth came early.*

He had survived again—this time. But how many more threats lay ahead?

❖

Reed doors rustled up and down the street as the men and older children came home from the fields.

Kebi set Tovyah on the blanket next to her and rose to go to the door. She opened it, expecting Amram to be on the other side, or close to it. He was nowhere in sight.

She looked down the road toward the gate. No one was in sight. Where was he? Accidents were common in the field. No formal notice ever came. Husbands—or sons—simply left for the day and never returned. She looked up and down. Puah's husband reached for his door.

She grabbed his arm. "Where is Amram?"

He shrugged. "He left our team today. He was moved to Joel's group."

Oh no. Her heart raced, her knees buckled. Joel had done nothing since Elli confronted her, but what would Joel do to Amram now that he was his overseer?

She looked west again. At the very end of the road she saw a lone figure.

Amram.

He shuffled slowly, as if every step brought him agony.

She looked back at Miriam, standing in the doorway. "Miriam, stay here with the boys. I'll be right back." She rushed toward him.

"Imma! What's wrong?"

"Just watch the baby," she called over her shoulder.

Her legs pumping as fast as possible, she soon reached him. "Amram, I was so afraid... You're so much later than all the others." She wrapped her arms around his neck, but he arched his back and groaned loudly. He gently grabbed her arms and pulled her away from him.

She scanned him from head to toe. Nothing seemed amiss—at first glance. "What's wrong? What happened?"

"Let's just get home, please."

She walked beside him, wishing she could alleviate his pain—whatever had caused it.

At their house she opened the door for him. He skipped washing and went into the common room and sat on the floor, his face contorted in pain.

She knelt beside him. "Amram, what happened?"

He was silent.

"What can I do for you?"

"Honey." He grunted.

Honey. Other than on bread, honey was for wounds. Cuts. Stripes from a lash.

She hurried to the room where their few supplies were stored and grabbed a pot of honey. She also grabbed a clean cloth and a bowl and poured a little water into it.

When she returned, he had removed his tunic and sat with his knees pulled up, his head on his knees. His back was covered in blood-crusted, wide red welts.

She gasped. Joel had to be responsible for this. Part of her wanted to race across the street to his house and pound him for being so cruel and vengeful.

But that would only make it worse.

She knelt behind him and dabbed beside each stripe, removing the dried blood as best she could without touching the raw flesh. The few times she failed, he hissed, pulling his back away from her for a moment, but remained silent.

When she had cleaned them as best she could, she removed the lid of the pot and dipped her fingers into the thick, golden liquid. Very gently, with as little pressure as possible, she smeared a thin layer of honey to each of his wounds.

"Let me get you something to eat."

"I'm not hungry."

"That may be, but you need to eat or you won't have the energy to make it through tomorrow."

He grunted his assent.

She hurried to the kitchen and scooped up a large bowl of barley stew. She poured him a cup of beer and returned to him.

She handed him the bowl and a piece of bread. After placing the cup on the floor, she sat next to him, as close as she dared.

Amram accepted the bowl and dipped his bread into it, soaking up the hot stew. His face was drawn, his shoulders hunched over, his eyes lifeless.

"Did Joel do this?"

He nodded, his mouth full.

"I thought you weren't in his group."

He swallowed. "I wasn't. He had me moved."

"So he could punish you?"

He shrugged.

"Did he give a reason for...doing this?" She couldn't bring herself to say the word *whip*.

"He said I was moving too slowly."

"I'm so sorry," she whispered.

His brow furrowed. "About what?"

She waved a hand at his back. "This. This is my fault. If I had…"

He gingerly set the bowl aside, then turned a soft gaze to her. "This is not your fault." His voice was strained. "We are slaves. We can be beaten at any time, for any reason or none at all. That is Egypt's fault. Joel used his power for selfish reasons. That is his fault. And it was the king who set all of this in motion with his ridiculous decree to destroy our children. There are any number of people who are responsible for this, but you are not one of them, ahuvati."

"Do you mean that, or are you trying to make me feel better?"

He smiled, and this time his eyes smiled as well as his mouth. "I mean it."

"But if we hadn't—"

"We obeyed God. I know what I heard. We had to do it. And if we suffer in order that our son may someday free us all, that is a price I am more than willing to pay."

She nodded. She had no other choice but to take him at his word.

While he finished his meal, she climbed to the roof and said good night to the children. She grabbed her mat and his, then brought them back downstairs and spread them out in the center of the common room near Tovyah.

Amram rolled onto his hands and knees and then lay down on his belly.

He wouldn't be sleeping on his back for a long time.

Kebi lay awake, trying to reason it all out. Things had turned out so much worse than she thought they might when Miriam took her to Beketaten. All she could think of then was how thankful she was to have Tovyah back, even if only for a while.

All of them had paid the price. Miriam spent a large part of her day doing what Kebi should be doing. Amram was punished for nonexistent infractions. And she was the object of glares from every woman who had lost a son in those horrible months. Only little Aaron was oblivious to the new disruptions in an already difficult life.

But what choice did she have? Any other option left her son most likely dead. She had obeyed God. There was no other option.

And she'd do it all over again.

CHAPTER TEN

✦

They made their lives bitter with harsh labor in brick and mortar and with all kinds of work in the fields; in all their harsh labor the Egyptians worked them ruthlessly.

~ Exodus 1:14 (NIV) ~

Kebi cringed as the door to Beket's rooms swung open, and the princess stormed through the open courtyard.

"Just because he is the king! He was my brother long before he was the king. I would have been king if I were a man." She continued muttering under her breath, but Kebi couldn't understand her rapidly spoken Egyptian.

With Tovyah in her arms, Kebi stepped back toward the wall, for a moment contemplating hiding behind one of the pillars that lined the open-air space.

"Neferet!" The frown on Beket's face spelled trouble for the servant. Lately, Neferet was never where she should be, and it seemed Beket was nearing the end of her patience.

After one more screech of her name, the handmaiden appeared and dipped her head.

"Where have you been?"

"I was doing the washing, nebet-i."

"You are to *oversee* the washing, not do it yourself. I need you available for me."

"Yes, nebet-i. I understand. But the washers seem to require constant supervision."

"Tell Maia. She'll see to it you have who and what you need."

Neferet bowed deeply. "Yes, nebet-i. Thank you. How may I assist you?"

"I want some juice and fresh fruit. Enough for two."

"Instantly, nebet-i." The servant scurried away.

She ordered for two. Was she expecting a visitor? "Should I go elsewhere, nebet-i?"

Beket frowned for just a moment. "Of course not. I want to see him. Why would you?" She neared Kebi and took Mose from her.

"You seem to be expecting a visitor."

"No, no visitor." She smiled. "Just you and me. And Mose." She laughed.

Neferet appeared with a tray of sliced cucumbers and cubes of watermelon in one hand and a pitcher of fruit juice in the other. She placed them on a table and returned to hover in the doorway.

Beket sat in one of the wide chairs placed on the portico and nodded toward the food while she settled Mose in her arms. "Go ahead. Eat. Try the melon."

Kebi reached for a piece of melon but pulled back her hand when Beket let out a gasp. "What?"

"You have blood on your sleeve!" She gestured to Kebi's arm. "Quite a bit of it."

Kebi twisted to look at the hem of her garment. Crimson scuffs were visible up to her elbow. How had she missed that? "I must have cut myself preparing the stew yesterday." A lie, but how could she tell her about Amram?

Beket beckoned to Neferet and handed her Mose, then stood and grabbed Kebi's hand. She shoved her sleeve up and examined her hands and forearms.

"The blood is not yours."

"It's all right. It's not a problem. Please don't concern yourself with me." Kebi tried to pull her arm back, but Beket wouldn't let go.

She straightened and placed her fists on her hips. "I most certainly do. If you are injured, you can't properly care for my son. Now, whose is it?" She fixed her gaze on Kebi.

She looked away. "Please, don't make me say it."

"Say what?"

"It's my...husband's."

"How did it end up on your tunic? What happened?" Her kohl-rimmed eyes wide, she released Kebi's arm.

"I was applying honey to his wounds."

"Wounds from...?"

"He was beaten."

"Badly, it appears. By whom?"

"His supervisor—his Israelite supervisor—did it."

"What did he do?"

"Nothing!"

"Then why was he punished?"

Beket crossed her arms. It was obvious the princess would not let it go until she was satisfied. "And?"

Might as well tell her all of it. What could it hurt? "The supervisor lives a few doors away from us. Their newborn son was thrown in the Nile about the same time ours was born. His wife confronted me after I first returned from here with Mose. She demanded to know who he was, why I had a living baby to care for, why I was in an Egyptian chariot."

"You should simply have told her the baby is mine and you are my menat."

This was a woman who had rarely, if ever, been denied anything. She couldn't fathom jealousy, because she had never been jealous. When she wanted something, she just took it.

"I did, but she became so upset, she struck me. Amram stepped between us, and then her husband saw the scuffle—"

"I do not understand why she was so upset."

How could Kebi make her understand such raw, illogical emotion? "Princess, what if you suddenly had to give Mose up? How would you feel?"

Her jaw dropped. "Who would do that? Who would dare take my child?"

"Then what if he became ill? Wouldn't you do anything to have him back, even for a day?"

The assuredness on her face slowly dissipated as Beket considered the loss of her only child.

She sat across from Kebi. "I understand," she whispered. "Please, continue."

"One week after the confrontation at the village gate, the overseer said, or rather announced to the entire team, that Amram had not met his quota of bricks, though it was clear he had from the pile beside him. Some of the women have told me their husbands attested to the fact that he had. But the supervisor's word is law. So he whipped my Amram, mercilessly." Her voice was nearly a whisper. "He's done it twice more since but not as badly. But since his other wounds had not yet healed, they still bled. He can barely sleep. Working reopens the wounds every day. I beg your forgiveness for appearing in your palace in an unclean tunic. I did not notice the blood."

Beket was silent for a long moment.

Had Kebi made a mistake in telling her?

"Do you think that is what bothers me? That I am more worried about your appearance than your safety?"

"I apologize again, nebet-i."

Beket jumped to her feet. "We shall simply have to have him moved to another workspace."

"No!"

The shock on Beket's face told Kebi she had overstepped her boundaries. She dropped to her knees at the princess's feet. "I'm so sorry, nebet-i. Please forgive me. I did not mean to be disrespectful."

Beket grasped Kebi's shoulders. "Please rise. But tell me why you don't want me to help."

Kebi took her seat again. "It will only make things worse."

"Worse?"

"My position in the village is already…precarious. There are others—a few—who feel as this man and his wife. They hate me for nursing an Egyptian prince."

Beket sighed. "If you insist, I will do nothing. This time. If it continues, I will take action."

"Yes, nebet-i."

"It is because I care about you. You should not be punished for my actions."

People were punished for her actions, and those of her family, every day. She just didn't see it.

And in the end, this wasn't punishment for Beket's actions, but for her own, no matter what Amram said. She had no control over their position as slaves, or what the king may decree, but she was the one who'd placed her son in a basket and shipped him downstream to the princess, whether that was her intention or not.

Would the retribution ever stop?

❖

Mahu waited outside the middle palace. He took Mose as she climbed into the chariot. "I see you have a new tunic."

How much did he know already? "Yes, Beket noticed I had blood on mine and gave me this one." She rubbed the hem of her sleeve between her thumb and finger. "It's so soft and white. It's made for a princess, not a slave."

"I think it suits you." He grinned and returned Mose to her before joining her on the platform.

"May I ask you a question?"

"Of course."

"You wear the bees around your neck. I know that is a rare honor given in battle. The men call you 'Captain,' but they act as though you are much more than a captain."

He chuckled. "Is that a question?"

"It just doesn't make sense to me. It's not my business, but I wondered if you would explain it to me."

"I earned the Award of Valor many years ago while I was Chief of the Medjay for Akhenaten. I discovered a plot to assassinate the king, and I prevented it from happening. The king rewarded me for saving his life."

Now on the causeway, Mahu commanded the horses to pick up their pace. "After Tut became king and moved the capital back to Waset, he asked me to continue. I told him I would be honored to continue guarding him and his family but that I'd decided I wanted something simple, where I would be home more. Because of my age, he decided to honor my request and made me chief of the palace Medjay. Officially, I'm a captain, under the chief, but many still treat me as if I were still chief."

"No wonder they respect you as they do. It sounds as though you deserve it."

"I'm not so sure about that. I succeeded that time, but eventually…" He clamped his mouth shut, as if he had said too much already.

He remained silent for a while, then turned to her. "It is my turn to ask a question."

Her stomach tightened. What could he want to know? The only secret she had could get her killed.

"May I ask how you were injured? Did it happen at the palace?"

"The blood wasn't mine. It was my husband's." She cringed. She hadn't meant to tell anyone, but Beket knew, and now Mahu would know too.

"What happened to him?"

Kebi resisted sighing. She told him about the beating.

"I'm sorry that happened to you both." He paused. "It's enough that you are mistreated by us. You should not have to endure it from your own people."

"I think at first, our people become supervisors to avoid the punishments themselves. Instead they pass it on to others."

"Slaves rarely need to be physically punished. There are better ways to motivate people. And to ensure obedience."

Or they could not be enslaved to begin with. But Mahu surely only knew what he had been taught, what he had known his whole life.

Just as she did.

Too bad the rest of the Egyptian nobility didn't share his opinions.

◆

Kebi was ready with hot stew and honey when Amram returned from work the next night. She met him at the door, expecting the same exhausted man who could barely move who had entered the house each night for the last week. Instead he kissed her, a broad smile gracing his face.

She placed her hand on his cheek and searched his eyes. "What happened? Why is your beautiful smile in its rightful place again?"

"I am no longer under Joel." He reached around her to place his sandals in the basket by the door. "I'm hungry."

Hunger was a good sign. He'd eaten so little these last days, his unending pain robbing him of appetite, sleep, and patience. Even little Aaron had learned to stay out of Abba's way.

She hurried to the back while he climbed to the roof to enjoy the cooler air. Why had he been moved? How? A sick feeling overwhelmed her. Had Beket managed this? What did the other men say when this happened? What did Amram think? At the moment, he was clearly pleased, but what would he say if he knew she had talked to Beket and the princess had interfered?

A pot of barley and root stew in hand, she climbed the stairs. Bowls and a stack of warm bread already waited.

"Thank you, ahuvati." He dipped his bread into the stew, scooping up a large mouthful.

Kebi waited until he had eaten about half the bowl. "What happened? Why were you moved?"

"I have no idea." He spoke around a mouthful of bread. "An Egyptian foreman came and asked for me as soon as I arrived. I thought perhaps Joel had spoken to his supervisor, and I was to be punished even more harshly. For a moment, I wondered if I would even return home." His face had a darkness she rarely saw.

"But instead he told me I was now to work with the counters." He shoved another bite into his mouth. "Joel was not happy I would no longer be under his control." The slightest smile briefly appeared.

"I can imagine. Who knows what he'll tell everyone."

"I hope this doesn't make things worse for him and Elli. I don't think there are many left who pity them. Not after the beatings. Many women have lost their sons, but no one takes it out on anyone else. Except them."

The pain Kebi had felt when the princess called Tovyah her son, held him and cooed at him, changed his name…that was nothing compared to what others were feeling. She needed to be patient with Elli.

But how far could patience go when it was met continually with rage, resentment, and retribution?

What did Elli have yet in store for them?

CHAPTER ELEVEN

◆

"Then 'a new king, to whom Joseph meant nothing, came to power in Egypt.' He dealt treacherously with our people and oppressed our ancestors by forcing them to throw out their newborn babies so that they would die."
~ Acts 7:18–19 (NIV) ~

TA-AABET, FIRST MONTH OF PERET, THE SEASON OF GROWING

Kebi watched the farmers bent over their fields as the chariot raced by. The Nile's life-giving waters had come and gone, leaving behind rich black soil. Wheat, barley, chickpeas, beans, corn, flax—all had to be in the ground soon if they were to have enough time to grow tall and bear fruit.

Days at the palace had settled into a comfortable routine over the last several months, or at least as comfortable as possible between slave and mistress. Beket always had a delicious morning meal ready for them when they arrived. Hot, soft wheat bread, juice or weak beer, fruit if in season. When the meal ended, Beket took Tovyah into her arms for a walk around the courtyard, showing him plants and flowers. Later she played with him in the main hall until he was hungry again. Kebi fed him, and then the princess laid him down for his nap. When he woke, the whole routine started over again.

Beket adored every moment of it. Kebi had begun bringing something to occupy her time while Tovyah was sleeping or with the princess—mending or sewing, usually.

Beket had left to bathe, the only time Kebi had Tovyah to herself for a while. She suckled him, and he finally fell into a fitful sleep. Cutting teeth always made it hard for him to get any rest.

She realized she had left the tunic she was mending on the portico. He was sound asleep and still couldn't roll over, so she thought it would be safe to hurry out there and retrieve it.

Tunic in hand, she headed back to Tovyah's room. As she neared, she heard whispers from within. She halted and listened. A woman's voice. Singing? The voice was low, sweet. But not Beket's—she'd never heard Beket sing to him before.

She stepped closer to the sound, pausing just outside the door.

Run away, you who come in darkness....

Who would be coming in darkness?

Do you come to kiss this child? I will not let you kiss him.

Do you come to soothe him? I will not let you soothe him.

Do you come to harm him? I will not let you harm him.

Kebi suppressed a gasp. Who was singing to her son about harm and kisses?

Do you come to take him away? I will not let you take him away from me.

Take him away? Her heart pounding, Kebi gathered her courage and stepped inside.

Maia.

From her place on the bed beside Tovyah, the old woman simply glared, then returned her attention to him.

Needing an explanation, Kebi hurried to her. "What are you singing about? Who is coming to harm him?"

The Great Royal Nurse stood. "You do not belong here. You are not Egyptian. If you were, you would know what I am singing about."

"Then tell me, so I will know."

"This is the lullaby that every Egyptian mother sings over her children. It is to scare off the evil spirits that sometimes come for them."

What evil spirits?

"You must go." Maia's dark eyes shot daggers as she continued her unblinking stare.

"But I—"

"No. No arguments. Gather your things and go. The princess has said I will care for the child now."

Kebi hesitated. Had Beket really said she was through?

"Now! Go." Maia's arm shot out toward the main room.

Hot tears gathered on Kebi's lashes as she slunk toward the couch and gathered her things. She reached for the small sack hung on a peg behind it and stuffed the mending inside. She stopped at the door on her way out. "May I—may I say goodbye first?"

"Be gone." Maia didn't even turn around.

The princess had told her to stay. But Maia had said Kebi reported to her, and Maia said to go. Who would be angrier if she disobeyed?

Kebi left Tovyah's room, walked through the main hall, and started down the hallway that led to the outer door, trying to stifle her sobs. She doubled over, one hand around her middle, the other leaning on the wall.

El Shaddai, why? Why did You tease me so? Why only a few months, just enough to prolong and deepen the pain? She'd said goodbye once. This time, it was worse.

She jumped as a hand landed on her back.

"Kebi?"

The voice of the princess cut through her grief.

"Kebi? What's wrong? Why are you here in the hall? Who is with Mose?" Her voice was laced with equal parts fear and concern, with a tinge of anger underneath.

"I was told"—she glanced backward—"I was told you no longer needed me. That another is to care for him."

"Who told you that?" Her eyes narrowed. "No one can tell me who I can and cannot hire. Not even my brother."

"I should go. I don't wish to cause trouble for anyone."

Beket rolled her eyes. "Maia."

Kebi remained silent. If Maia knew she had revealed their conversation to Beket, who knew what she would do?

"I'll take care of Maia. You'll stay." She led Kebi to a chair in the main hall. "Wait here. I'll be back." She marched off.

After a few moments, Maia came toward her, Beket behind her.

"I apologize. Please return to the child's side." Her words held an apology but not her eyes.

Kebi glanced at Beket, who nodded. She dried her eyes. "I am truly sorry for whatever I have done to offend you."

Confusion flared in Maia's eyes for a brief moment, but they turned cold just as quickly.

"Good then. Tend to my son." Beket left Kebi and Maia standing there in an awkward silence.

Maia raised her chin. "Just remember who is the Egyptian of noble blood and who is a worthless slave, and we'll get along."

Remembering would be easy. It wasn't likely Maia would ever let her forget.

◆

"Just a little more...you can do it. Keep going." Kneeling next to him on the hard dirt floor in their home, Kebi clasped her hands at her chest to keep from helping Tovyah turn from his back to his tummy.

He'd been trying for six or seven days. He'd mastered rolling from tummy to back in a day, but going the other way was proving more difficult.

He squirmed and grunted, hands waving and feet kicking. He pulled his feet up and rolled to his side but couldn't quite push himself over his arm. He flopped to his back.

"Try again, motek."

He apparently was happy on his back for the moment. He chewed on his fist, eyes darting all around, to her, to the sky above, to the wall. So much to see for such a small baby.

He'd try again when he was ready. She picked up the basket she'd been weaving.

A few moments later, he stretched his arms out. He rolled to his side, arched his back, and landed on his tummy.

Kebi cheered. No matter how many children, how many accomplishments, every time was joyous. "Such a big boy!"

It took him a brief moment to free his arm, which was caught under his chest. He raised his head to look up at her, a crooked but triumphant grin on his face.

She helped him onto his back. Within moments he found himself on his tummy again.

Tovyah soon wore himself out rolling back and forth.

Kebi picked him up and scooted back against the wall, knees pulled up slightly. She laid him on her legs, his feet to her chest, his little fists grasping her fingers.

"How about a story? What shall I tell you today?" She thought a moment, remembering which tales of their ancestors she had shared with him most recently. "How about Joseph? He is the reason we're here, after all."

Tovyah cooed, as if urging her to go on.

"Father Jacob had twelve sons. He had four wives, so I guess twelve sons isn't that surprising." She laughed, and he laughed with her. "But Joseph was the first son of his favorite wife, and he loved him more than the others. One day Jacob gave Joseph a beautiful coat, a richly embroidered robe made of the softest material Jacob could buy. It made his brothers jealous, and they attacked him and sold him to a caravan, which brought him here to Egypt."

Tovyah put his fist in his mouth, bright eyes never leaving her face.

"Yes, it was a good life for a very long time. The king loved Joseph and gave him control of the entire kingdom. Then a terrible famine struck Canaan. Jacob sent his sons to buy grain here. Joseph recognized them, and eventually he brought his whole family to live here in the delta, where it is lush and fertile."

Shiphrah poked her head in the door.

"Shiphrah, come join us."

The midwife quietly came to sit beside her. "Finish your story."

"After a long time, a new king came to power. He didn't care about Joseph's family, and he moved us from the delta to the cities and forced us to make bricks to build his temples and his palaces." She swallowed the resentment building in her throat. "And then he decided there were too many of us, and he made us work harder and longer. But Shaddai still allowed us to multiply."

She rubbed her free fingers against his cheek. "King Tut is afraid of you, motek. He doesn't know who you are, but if he finds out, he will try to do everything in his power to destroy you. But Shaddai will protect you, just as He has so far. The edict could not harm you, the river could not swallow you, the astrologer could not hurt you. And I will not allow the princess to hurt you either, by filling your head with stories of false gods. I will tell you of the one true God, the living God who created you, and He has promised that one day you will remember the truth. I will stay by your side until I am certain nothing will come against you."

They sat silently for a while. Then Shiphrah wrapped an arm around her shoulders. "Let me ask you something. Do you truly believe everything you are telling him?"

Kebi winced. "I'm trying, Shiphrah. I really am. But it's so very hard. It would be easier to believe I can make the Nile change directions and flow the other way."

Shiphrah squeezed her shoulder.

"Amram has so much faith. He truly believes, with every breath he takes—and Miriam does too, for that matter—that Shaddai will protect Tovyah and keep him safe from both the Egyptians and their false gods. Why can't I believe?" She sniffled. "I must be a terrible mother."

"No, my friend. It is *because* you are such a devoted mother that you find it hard to believe. El Shaddai has given you a mother's heart. You love your children with a ferocity I have rarely seen. You give your whole being to them. It is your job to keep them safe, and you would do anything to accomplish that."

If *anything* included putting a baby in a basket in a flowing river, then yes.

"It's that fierce love that keeps you from seeing anything else. You think you are the one who should protect him, care for him, love him."

What a ridiculous statement! Kebi turned to the midwife. "Of course I am the one. Who else should do it?"

"You are one but not the only one."

"I don't understand. Are you saying the princess is the one to love and care for him?"

"I'm not saying that, though that is not for me to decide. Or you. I am saying that there are others, right here, who love him as much."

"If Amram loves him as I do, how can he even think of giving him away? This is his son, his flesh, his blood."

Shiphrah smiled. "Because Amram can see beyond these walls, beyond today. Beyond his heart. If Shaddai has told him that this baby, his son, will save the Israelites from the Egyptians, how can he not let him go?"

Kebi tried to see "beyond." But no matter how hard she tried, she couldn't get past the idea of letting him go.

◆

For once Kebi was eager to get to the palace, to show Beket Tovyah's newfound skill. She dressed him in the linen tunic Beket had sent home with him. A prince could never be seen dressed in wool.

She jumped from the chariot as soon as it pulled up to the door. The guards admitted her, and she hurried down the hall to the main room.

Beket came to greet them, as she always did. "Come here, *habibi*." She reached for Tovyah, but Kebi stopped her. "I have to show you what he can do now." She set him on the tiled floor on his back. "He did it the first time three days ago, and since then he's become quite good at it."

Tovyah kicked and turned over.

"Isn't that marvelous?"

Beket smiled. "Yes, it's wonderful." Why did she sound so defeated? A strange reaction. She was fascinated by everything he did, reciting his every action and sound to Kebi as if she had never been around a child.

Beket remained subdued throughout the morning. After Kebi fed Tovyah and laid him on his ornate bed for his nap, the princess entered the room.

Kebi backed away, tying the neck of her tunic closed.

Beket sat beside him. She liked to rub his back as he fell asleep. "My son."

Tovyah sucked his thumb.

"I wish I had seen you a few days ago, when you were trying so hard to roll over. You're very good now, but I would have liked to see you the first time. I'm sorry I'm not with you every day. Right now I can't give you what you need, but one day we'll be together as we should be, and I'll get to see all the amazing things you do."

Kebi's heart clenched. She'd been so excited about Tovyah that she hadn't even considered Beket.

Or had she? Had she helped Tovyah roll over at home just to keep Beket from enjoying his triumphs?

Was this Kebi's way of still claiming Tovyah as her son, and not Beket's?

CHAPTER TWELVE

❖

"I am God Almighty; walk before me faithfully and be blameless."
~ Genesis 17:1 (NIV) ~

APEP, THIRD MONTH OF SHEMU, THE SEASON OF HARVEST

Kebi wove Miriam's curly brown tresses into a fat braid, then tied a small length of papyrus around the end to keep it in place. "Finished." She leaned forward and placed a kiss on her daughter's cheek.

Miriam turned around. "Thank you, Imma." She pulled up one knee to stand, but paused. "Imma?"

"Yes, motek?"

"Aaron is almost four, and Tovyah is almost one."

"Yes."

"Why am I not almost eight?"

"You will be, after the inundation."

Miriam screwed her mouth into a pout. "Why must I wait?"

"Because you were born at the beginning of planting season, but the boys were born in the third month of the harvest."

She huffed. "All right."

"What is it, motek?"

"When does Aaron have to join the other boys and help with the bricks?"

"After his seventh year."

"That's not long, is it?"

"Three more years."

Miriam blinked rapidly. "At least he will come home every night with Abba. When Tovyah leaves...I will miss him." She stood and trudged away.

How long would Tovyah be allowed to live in the village? It was becoming painfully clear that Beket missed him, that once every ten days was not enough. Would she require Kebi to come more often? Or would she just take him away altogether, get an Egyptian woman to take over? The position of menat nesut was highly sought after, even among the wives of important and influential men. Usually only women such as Maia, already familiar with palace routines and behaviors, were chosen as royal nurses. Not someone like her.

Aaron scrambled off his sleeping mat and walked toward her. "Come here, my son."

He climbed into her lap and promptly fell asleep.

How would he ever be awake enough in the mornings to go to the brickfields?

At least she didn't have to worry about that for another three years.

That wasn't true when it came to Tovyah, however. A woman who had never wanted for anything would decide how long—or even if—Kebi would keep Tovyah. He could be taken from her any day.

She tried to believe Shaddai was in control. But between Maia and Beket, it was getting harder every day.

◆

Kebi held her breath as Tovyah let go of the grain jar he clung to.

He balanced himself, lifted one foot. Then *plop*. Right onto his bottom.

His eyes grew wide, and he looked to his imma to see whether he should laugh or cry.

Kebi laughed. "You're all right. Try again." She picked him up and set him on his feet. Balancing, he thought for a moment, then dropped back to his hands and knees to crawl into the main room.

"He was walking! Why did he stop?" Miriam frowned. "I'll go pick him up again."

"No, motek. Leave him alone. A baby doesn't learn to walk all at once. Right now, it's still much easier and faster for him to crawl. He'll keep trying, and eventually he'll be as good at walking as you are." She returned to the cooking area at the back of the house. "Can you watch him and make sure he doesn't get hurt?"

"Yes, Imma." Miriam darted off.

Kebi sat on her knees before the quern. Unable to sleep last night, she'd ground the day's grain and now had time to make the bread before she left. She picked up the dough she'd been kneading, turned it over, and leaned into it. After a few more times, she pulled off a small ball of the mixture and flattened it between her palms, pressing it into one hand and then the other. When it had reached a suitable size, she opened the small door on the side of the beehive-shaped oven. She jerked her head back as heat whooshed out, then slapped the disc on the inside of the small oven.

She continued forming the flatbread, adding new pieces and removing those already cooked. Soon a large stack of warm, soft bread waited in a basket, covered by a cloth. She stirred the barley and onion stew already in a large pot over the firepit. It would simmer all day while she was at the palace. Amram would at least have a filling, hot meal when he returned from the brickfields.

Miriam giggled in the front room. Kebi looked over her shoulder to see her placing Tovyah once again on his feet. Hands out to his sides, he balanced perfectly. One foot lifted and set in front of the other. Before he could shift his weight to it, Kebi swooped in and picked him up.

"Why did you do that? He was ready to take a step." Miriam stared up at her with wide eyes.

Beket's disappointed face was still seared in her mind from months ago, when Kebi told her he had rolled over. She had determined not to do that again, and all week she had kept him from taking that crucial first step.

As much as it killed her.

Noise behind her drew her attention to little Aaron, coming down from the roof.

"Good morning, motek." Kebi knelt to gather him in her arms as well and squeezed tightly. "I love you, my son."

Aaron squirmed out of her embrace. "Today I stay with Nathanael?"

"Yes. Is that all right?"

"Yes!" His dark eyes sparkled. "His imma makes sweet bread!"

Kebi forced a smile. Knowing he preferred Shiphrah to her only because of the honey her earnings as a midwife allowed them did not ease the sting.

"It's time for us to go. Kiss me goodbye." She leaned over so Aaron could reach her cheek, then stood, kissing Miriam. "Take care of Aaron."

"Yes, Imma."

Kebi strolled down the road to the eastern end, where Mahu leaned against the chariot, waiting.

He pushed off, his arms out to hold Tovyah as she climbed into the chariot. He placed her son back into her arms, then jumped up beside her. He commanded the horses, and the chariot was on its way.

"How is the little prince today?" Mahu smiled down at Tovyah.

"Almost walking. I'm hoping today he will take his first steps so the princess will see."

He flashed her an approving smile. "That will make her very happy."

"I know."

The sand stretched out to the east, running up to the small mountains. Barely visible in the distance were the tombs of the kings, of Akhenaten and his father, Amenhotep III. Their wives and children. Work on Tut's tomb had already begun. Massive memorials to the men who claimed to be gods.

El Shaddai, guard Tovyah's heart.

The gates opened before them, and Mahu expertly guided the horses to Beket's door.

"Thank you." Kebi smiled at the man who reminded her so much of her abba, then turned to enter the palace.

Beket greeted them at the door. "Mose, habibi!" She held out her arms, and he went willingly into them.

"I'm so happy to see you." Beaming, Beket glanced at Kebi. "Both of you. Come, I have some wonderful fresh figs. They're quite sweet this year."

Kebi dutifully followed Beket outside into the shade of the courtyard. A plate of fresh sliced figs sat next to a pitcher of juice.

Miu slept peacefully in one chair but hopped up at their approach. She wandered between and around Kebi's legs. Kebi stiffened. She still hadn't become used to the idea of animals running free in a home.

Beket sat and settled Tovyah on her lap, but he immediately squirmed away onto the floor. She laughed. "He still likes to walk around tables, I see."

"He's very close to walking. He may do it today."

Beket's face lit up like a summer dawn. "Oh, that would be so wonderful. His first steps, right here in his home."

It's not his home—yet.

"Let's see if he will do it." Kebi moved him away from the furniture and stood behind him. She bent and grabbed his little fists.

He gained his balance and then, just as he had done a hundred times this week, moved one foot forward.

A Mother's Sacrifice: Jochebed's Story

Kebi let go.

Tovyah took four more steps before falling to the tile floor and crawling quickly away, sending Miu scampering off.

The *sat nesut's* eyes glistened. "Thank you," she whispered.

Why *thank you*? Did she realize what Kebi had done? Hopefully not. If she did, she'd wonder why. Maybe ask questions Kebi had no answer for. "You're welcome."

Beket jumped up to help him take a few more steps. Every time he did, Beket clapped her hands, laughing and smothering him with kisses.

Kebi could do nothing but sit and smile.

At the end of the day, after walking off and on, getting as far as eleven steps in a row, Tovyah was exhausted. So was Kebi. Keeping emotions bottled up took more energy than she'd expected.

She'd done the right thing. Beket should experience his triumphs if she was going to raise him.

Kebi should feel better than she did. She should feel proud of herself.

Instead, she felt like a piece of herself was missing.

◆

Kebi submersed the water jug, filled it, and set it aside. The river had not yet begun to rise, according to the stone marker one of the Egyptian farmers nearby had placed on his land.

She reached for the other jug and shoved it beneath the water. Bubbles rose to the surface as water replaced air. *Glug, glug, glug.*

In Egypt, life revolved around the river and its annual gift of a flood. The priests had special buildings with steps spiraling down to keep track of the water's level as it rose day by day. Great pains were taken to examine the river daily, sometimes hourly, to determine when Isis's tears began to overflow the Nile. Once begun, the worry did not stop.

If Isis did not cry enough, only part of the cropland would be covered. Only a part would be gifted the fertile earth the Nile left when she pulled her waters back. Only a part of the food necessary to feed this massive nation would be grown, and famine would result.

But if the goddess was missing her murdered husband more than usual, the water would sweep away villages, dams, and canals. The raging river would drown not only livestock, but people. In extreme circumstances the water would not recede in time, preventing the crops from even being planted at all until it was too late.

That had not happened since the Israelites had come to Egypt. She'd heard that records showed the river had once nearly destroyed the land, but Egypt survived, as she had for hundreds of years. Under Amenhotep, Egypt had been at the height of her glory. No wars were needed, because he had made peace with all their neighbors.

Then his son Akhenaten took over and turned the country upside down. He'd insisted everyone worship only the Aten. He'd been obsessed with his new religion and neglected all else. Much territory had been lost. Many were sure he had been assassinated to stop the downward slide he'd led Egypt into.

And now his son ruled them, a child who wanted Kebi's son dead.

She picked up the now-heavy pottery jugs, balanced them in her arms, and headed for home. She sucked in a deep breath of air smelling of river and dust. This was her favorite time of year. The air was beginning to warm up a bit, keeping the nights from becoming so cold, but the days weren't unbearably hot yet.

A year ago, Tovyah had burst into the world. If she were lucky, she would get one more year with him. Possibly two.

The rich Egyptians held feasts to mark the day of their birth. Elaborate offerings of food, flowers, and candles were made to the gods. Goose and cow, spiced and sweetened with honey, were served. Plates filled with fruit, chickpeas, lentils, lettuce, and cucumbers were passed around along with baskets of breads, cakes, and biscuits. They would eat—and waste—more food in a day than the village would eat in a month.

The Israelites saw no reason for such extravagance. If a particular day was remembered at all, and not just a time of year, the day was quietly noted, and Shaddai was praised, especially when a young child had lived for another year.

This time last year Kebi wasn't sure Tovyah would even live a year.

Thank You, El Shaddai, for keeping him safe thus far.

What did the next year hold?

◆

After another long day at the palace, Kebi waited outside the door for Mahu to take her home. The chariot waited, but he was nowhere to be seen. Why was he late? It wasn't like him.

The door guards were beginning to eye her. Tovyah was getting fussy, tired of being held, but she couldn't let him walk around out here. Slaves were not permitted to wander around the palace unescorted. Maybe she should see if she could find out what was keeping Mahu. Tovyah on her hip, she gestured to the door, and one of the Medjay let her back in. She crept to the end of the entranceway and peered around the corner. No one in sight. She moved to the doors to the hall, pulled one open a hand's breadth.

She could hear Mahu's low voice. He stood near the doors. With Maia.

They didn't look happy.

Maia glared up at the much taller man, arms crossed. Kebi had seen that stance before, and it was not a good sign.

Mahu stomped away a few strides, then stormed back to her. "No! *Nen, nen, nen!* I said I didn't, and you're going to have to trust me."

"But I heard—"

"I don't care what you heard." He reached for her hands, held them as he looked tenderly at her. "How long have we been together? Nearly all our lives, and I have never lied to you."

Maia studied him a long moment, then dropped her head. She mumbled something to Mahu, and he pulled her into his arms.

Kebi hurried back outside as quietly as she could.

How could that sweet man be married to such a horrible woman?

The door was yanked open, and Mahu appeared. He strode to the chariot and helped her up. He hopped on, belted a command, and they lunged ahead.

After they had cleared the palace, the muscles in his neck and shoulders appeared to relax. After a few moments more, he turned to Kebi. "I know you saw us. Maia and me." His voice held no anger, no accusation.

Still, her cheeks heated.

"I'm sorry, I didn't mean to spy on you. I was only trying to find out where you were. You're never late. I didn't know what to do."

"I know." He cleared his throat. "I suppose you have realized Maia is my wife."

That much was clear. What she couldn't understand was how he put up with her sullen, argumentative, commanding attitude every day.

He let out a long breath. "Neither of us approved of Tut's decree to kill the children. Maia cried for days, not only for the children who would be lost, but for Tut. She practically raised him. She begged him to reconsider. It cut her very deeply."

Kebi had never seen the first hint of any softness in Maia. But to be trusted as the Great Royal Nurse, to suckle the crown prince, she must have goodness in her somewhere.

"Someone just told her I had been sent to the village last year, participated in the purge of the long-tailed star. She had no reason to distrust this person, so she assumed I had helped the others kill the babies. She couldn't believe I would do that, and she was right. I didn't. I never could have. But I did search the houses, so it wouldn't be so obvious I hadn't obeyed. She heard the others talking about me and came to the wrong conclusion. It tore her apart, thinking I had done that."

"Does she believe you?"

"She does now. After she calmed herself, she realized I could never have done that. She had to decide whether to trust what she knew from loving me all these years or listen to idle chatter, and she decided to believe her heart."

At the edge of the village, he pulled the horses to a stop, and she climbed down.

He leaned toward her. "I know you don't see the Maia I know. But no matter what it looks like, you must know that everything she does, she does for the children. She truly does want the very best for them."

She nodded. "Good night, Mahu."

"*Shem en hotep.*"

The chariot wheels rumbled away as she slipped inside the walls.

Had Mahu recognized her as the mother whose baby he let live? If he had, he had never given her any indication of it. Would he eventually place her as that mother, Tovyah as that baby?

And if he did, what would he do?

CHAPTER THIRTEEN

They sacrificed to false gods, which are not God—gods they had not known, gods that recently appeared, gods your ancestors did not fear.
~ Deuteronomy 32:17 (NIV) ~

DYEHUTY, FIRST MONTH OF AKHET, THE SEASON OF INUNDATION

Kebi set Tovyah on the tile floor when they entered Beket's palace, and he toddled ahead. He'd been walking for two months but his steps were still wobbly.

"How is our little one this morning?" Beket hurried toward them.

"A little fussy. He has more teeth coming in."

"Then we'll have to see what we can do to make him think of something else." She took his hand and led him to the chairs on the portico. Three were set out now instead of two. Tovyah clambered onto one and turned around to a seated position. He stretched his hands to try to rest them on the arms, as Beket did, but he couldn't reach them.

Beket laughed as she sat in the chair beside him. She reached to tickle his tummy, setting off a flurry of giggles. "Do you know what this week is, habibi? One year ago I found you in your basket in the river. Can you believe it's been a whole year?"

Kebi silently thanked Shaddai. One day a week was a small price to pay to have him near her for a year, to have him alive and healthy. Happy.

A young woman Kebi had never seen brought their morning meal. She set a platter of sliced fruit and a pitcher on the table and turned to go, but Beket grabbed her hand. "Hannah, I want you to meet Jochebed. She is Hebrew too." She turned to Kebi. "Hannah is my new handmaiden. Neferet said we needed more help."

"I'm so glad to know you're here. I won't feel as lonely." Hannah smiled brightly.

Such a pretty girl. She reminded Kebi of someone, but she couldn't place her.

Beket pointed to the kitchens. "See Neferet. She'll tell you what to do next."

"Yes, nebet-i." She grabbed the platter and disappeared.

Beket studied Kebi a moment. "I have to tell you something."

"Me?" Kebi pointed to her chest. Beket talked to Tovyah so much it was sometimes difficult to tell when she was addressing someone else.

Beket nodded. "Next month my brother is celebrating the Festival of Opet. It used to be the grandest, most opulent festival of all, but since it is to worship Amun, my father stopped it. Tut, or more likely Vizier Ay, wants to revive it. They've been restoring the temples across the river for the last three years, and Ay has declared them ready. Tut wants me there—with Mose, as a prince."

Kebi nodded. "It sounds like a wonderful time."

"It is a wonderful time." She glanced around and leaned near. "Even if they are worshipping a false god," she whispered.

Her admission shocked Kebi. *She* knew they were idols, but why would Beket say that? "Why are they false? I mean, why do *you* think they are?"

"At this ceremony, the god Amun, his consort Mut, and their son Khonsu, are taken from the northern temple upriver to the southern temple. There, they consummate, again"—she rolled her eyes—"their union to ensure the fertility of the land. Then their power is reignited, and some of it is transferred to the king." She shook her head. "I know my father was right. There is only one god, the god who created everything. The Aten."

She had the right idea but the wrong god. She was still worshipping a false god, the sun disk, a creation of Shaddai. Perhaps someday Kebi could introduce her to the living God, the Creator.

"You might not like it though." Beket winced.

"And why might I not like it?"

"It lasts fifteen days—on the other side of the river."

Kebi felt like the floor had opened up under her. The problem immediately became clear. She couldn't go fifteen days without allowing Tovyah to suckle. Her milk would dry up in days.

Was it now time to finally say goodbye to him? To allow Beket to be his mother in every way?

She paused while she steadied her voice. "I understand. Do you want me to come until the day before you leave, or would you like me to leave now?"

Beket frowned. "Why would you leave?"

"I cannot continue to be his nurse after being apart fifteen days. I won't be able to come back."

Her face brightened. "No, you misunderstand. I don't want you to come back. I want you to come with us. I want you to continue to be his menat. Mose loves you. I don't know what he'd do without you. Or what I would do, for that matter."

Solid ground reappeared, but joy was immediately replaced by hesitation. What would Aaron and Miriam do without her for that long? Amram wouldn't like her to be absent from him for that many days.

Did being present with part of her family mean deserting the rest?

◆

Kebi cringed at Amram's scowl. She'd waited until the children had gone up to the roof before bringing up what she knew would be a difficult conversation. She'd expected him to be unhappy but not this upset.

"Fifteen days?" He threw his hands up. "What are we supposed to do without you for *fifteen days?*"

"Shiphrah said she'd be happy to help with Miriam and Aaron. They can play with her children during the day, and she'll help with the evening meal."

He huffed. "That's what *you* are supposed to do. Not her."

"I'm sorry."

A frowned marred his usually calm face as he thought. "Can't someone else go instead?"

She shook her head. How could he ask that? He'd watched her nurse and wean two children before Tovyah. How was it men were always so ignorant about such simple things?

"If I don't feed him for that long, I won't be able to when he returns. We might as well say goodbye now if I do that." She glanced at Tovyah sleeping peacefully on a mat, knees pulled under his tummy, hands under his chest, a crooked smile on his face. She was not ready to say goodbye.

Fists on his hips, head down, Amram silently paced for several long moments. At the end of the long room, he halted, gazing down on his son. He blew out a breath, shaking his head.

Kebi's heart sank. Surely he'd have said something before now if he intended to allow her to go.

She could see his point. Rather, points. Fifteen days was a very long time—over two Israelite weeks. It took both a husband and wife to manage a home. Before they were made slaves, the men spent their days taking care of their large flocks, raising the year's crops, keeping the house in good repair. Now, with them in the brickfields any time the sun was up, most of that work was transferred to the women. And when just grinding the grain could take half a day, every day, precious little time remained to cook the bread, prepare a stew, water the straggly vegetables clinging to life along the wall, not to mention making and mending clothes and carrying water back from the river.

He paused, looked up. "We can manage without you for fifteen days. As long as you can stay with him, you should."

"Are you sure?"

"No, but what's the worst that could happen?" A bit of a grin revealed his dimple.

"I can tell her I can't go, if you like."

"Shaddai will take care of us. Of all of us. Go." He kissed her cheek. "I'm going up. Coming?"

"In a moment." She grabbed a small jug of water and poured some around the cumin, onion, and garlic plants growing outside the back wall. She filled the jug again and watered the cucumbers and radishes. In the summer sun, without water, they would quickly die. They needed attention every day.

Much like her children.

If she didn't go, who would tell Tovyah about Shaddai after he'd spent the day worshipping in the temples of false gods?

But leaving the others for so long? Was this a good idea?

Not for the first time, she wished she had Amram's faith.

◆

Kebi placed her hands on her hips and returned Maia's glare. "No, I won't do it. I won't sing the lullaby to him." Tovyah sat on his bed, silently watching the two women who so often violently disagreed on how to best care for him. Maia had instructed Kebi to sing the song when she readied him for a nap, and Kebi had refused.

"You refuse to obey?"

Though the older woman was a head shorter, Kebi nonetheless cringed before her. "I said only that I cannot sing the lullaby. I will follow any other orders you have for me. But to sing this song, to speak directly to evil spirits and ghosts—that would cause me to disobey my God, and that I cannot do."

Maia scoffed. "What kind of god does not allow you to sing? This is preposterous. Everyone sings."

"It is not the singing that is a problem. It is speaking to spirits that is forbidden."

"How are you to tell them to go if you are not allowed to speak to them? That doesn't even make sense."

"Instead of speaking to them directly, we ask God to keep them away from us. He is more powerful than they are, and He is certainly more powerful than we are. Talking to them ourselves just invites their participation in our lives."

"They are already participating in your life! Why do you think bad things happen to you? They happen because the evil spirits attack." Maia chuckled, as if at a small child who could not comprehend why he fell after running headlong downhill.

"I don't know why bad things happen." Kebi looked at Tovyah, sitting on his bed peacefully playing with a carved ivory horse. "I only know that El Shaddai has promised to be with us when they do."

Maia burst out in loud laughter. "Well, he must not be a very good god. He hasn't done much for your people lately. Perhaps your god is a slave to our gods, much as your people are slaves to us. Maybe if he can free himself, then he'll be able to help you. A bit."

Kebi's cheeks heated. How was she supposed to answer such a charge? Especially when she did not understand why El

Shaddai had remained silent for over four hundred years. Many of her people had given up expecting the Almighty to rescue them. They had begun worshipping the Egyptian gods, abandoning Shaddai altogether.

Her abba had remained faithful even when most of those around him had not, and he had taught her to do the same. Still, she had no answer to give Maia.

"Mose is Egyptian now. You have to get used to that. He is no longer an Israelite and will not be worshipping the Israelite god. He is an Egyptian prince. He will be expected to make sacrifices to Amun, and Mut, and all the other gods that rule our lives and have made us the most powerful nation ever."

Her words pricked Kebi's heart. She watched him giggle as he made the little horse run across the bed. Her beautiful baby boy would grow up to rule over his own people. Would he even know he'd been born an Israelite?

She had to rely on the words that El Shaddai had given Amram—that in time, Tovyah would remember everything she had taught him. Her job, then, was not to worry about his remembering what she had taught him but instead to teach him everything she could before she was swept from his life.

She turned back to Maia. "I understand that, but just as you have to be faithful to your gods, I must be faithful to the living God. I can't—and won't—stop you from singing the lullaby, but I can't do it myself."

Maia sneered. "You are weak, as all your people are weak. That is why you serve us and not the other way around."

"You may be right, but that is not my problem. I can only obey what I know to be true."

"Go then, and let me protect this child." She waved her hand in dismissal.

Kebi bent to place a soft kiss on Tovyah's cheek. "Sleep well."

He reached his little hands up to grab her neck and gave her a long hug.

Turning so Maia couldn't see the tears in her eyes, she left her son, beseeching El Shaddai to take care of him in her absence.

◆

"She was so harsh. You wouldn't believe the things she said about Shaddai. About us." Kebi cringed all over again at the thought of Maia's hateful words.

"Ahuvati, I've worked in the brickfields my entire life, with Egyptian overseers. I can surely imagine what she said." Amram grinned. "And I also imagine she used much more polite words to say it."

Kebi scooped out stew into bowls. "I've tried so hard to be pleasant, to obey everything else she has asked. But I think she just hates me. Hates all Israelites."

"May I suggest it has more to do with power than what people you are?" He picked up the jug of weak beer and a stack of pottery cups.

"What does that mean?"

"It means that even if you were Egyptian, Maia would still probably be upset with you just because you aren't doing as she asks. She has the authority. She wants you to respect it."

"Are you saying I should sing this despicable lullaby?" She loaded the flatbread in a basket and followed Amram up the steps.

"Of course not. But be extra careful not to say anything that sounds the slightest bit disrespectful."

"I wasn't rude. I simply told her why I couldn't sing it."

He set the jug down and handed Miriam and Aaron each a cup. "I'm very sure you didn't mean to be rude. But what you meant and what she heard could be two very different things. What you meant as just stating your beliefs she could take as you contradicting her."

"I guess."

"And saying I'm sorry, even if you didn't mean to be hurtful or disrespectful, never hurts. If she has been offended, even if you didn't mean to offend, an apology is never a bad idea."

Kebi had never thought of it that way. She ran through the entire conversation, looking for where she might have offended Maia.

From now on she would have to choose her words very carefully.

CHAPTER FOURTEEN

"Moses was educated in all the wisdom of the Egyptians and was powerful in speech and action."
~ Acts 7:22 (NIV) ~

PAENIPAT, SECOND MONTH OF AKHET, THE SEASON OF INUNDATION

When Kebi had left the palace two days ago, she'd been told she was expected to return there tonight so they could leave as soon as the sun rose. One more night away from Amram and the children.

She folded the new linen tunics the princess had given her to wear and placed them in the bottom of the sack. She wrapped a string tightly around the top and left it near the door, glancing down the street beyond the gate as she did. The sun almost kissed the tops of the western mountains, and soon Mahu would be waiting.

When she turned back, Miriam stood in the opposite corner watching her like a falcon following a field mouse. Her quivering lip was almost more than Kebi could stand.

"Come here." Kebi sat on the floor and patted her lap.

Miriam crawled into her lap in a way she hadn't done for years.

"I'm sorry, motek. I don't like it either. But it's not forever, it's only for a little while."

"But why do you have to go so far away?"

"It's just across the river. A very short journey."

"Can't they go without you, and then you can go back to the palace when they return?"

How did she explain milk production to a child? "No, that won't work. The day I stop going there is the last day any of us will ever see him. So I want to remain his nurse for as long as I can. I want to teach him as much about El Shaddai as I can before I have to let him go. I want to hold him as often as possible. I want… I just want to be his imma for as long as I can."

Miriam's little mouth twisted into a frown. "Won't you still be his imma, even if he's not here?"

"No, motek. The princess will be his imma."

"I don't understand. Won't you love him anymore?"

Kebi's heart shattered into a thousand pieces. "Do you think I would forget you or not love you if you weren't here?"

Miriam shook her head, dark curls bouncing.

"And I won't forget him or stop loving him. I will think about him every day for as long as I live."

Miriam pondered this. "I still hate it."

"So do I, motek. So do I."

"Will we ever see him again?"

Kebi shrugged. "I don't know. Shaddai did not tell us we would."

"You mean we'll really never see him again? Ever?" Her voice broke as the eventuality of their situation finally dawned on her. Before the river, while they hid him at home, it was almost a game to her. And every week when Kebi took him to Beket, Miriam played little mother, in charge of her brother, making the bread. She'd probably never really thought about what it would be like to lose him for good.

"Remember the story of Joseph? The reason our people came here to begin with?"

"Joseph was sold because his brothers were jealous." Miriam recited the story in a monotone. "So they sent him away."

"That's right."

She bolted up in Kebi's lap. "But I'm not jealous of Tovyah! I don't want him to go away."

"I know. But Joseph's brothers did, so they sold him to a caravan that brought him to Egypt. And once he arrived here, he was accused of doing something wrong, which he didn't do, and he was put in prison for many, many years. I'm sure he, at times, thought he would never get out. But when it was the right time, El Shaddai rescued him from the prison, and he was made the king's helper."

"And then he saved his family and all of Egypt!"

Kebi chuckled. "Yes, he did. And Shaddai has said your baby brother will save all Israel. I don't know when and I don't know how, but we must trust in that."

"Yes, Imma. I'll try."

Kebi tucked a tousled lock behind Miriam's ear. "It's hard, I know. But we mustn't stop hoping. If we have no hope, we have nothing."

"All right. I'll keep hoping, but I'll miss you and Tovyah while you're gone." She hopped off Kebi's lap and crossed the room to her brother. She leaned in and placed a sweet kiss on his head. "Goodbye, Tovyah."

For all her happy words, though, Kebi was hanging on to her own hope by a thread.

❖

Was the queasiness in her stomach the result of the boat's rolling from side to side or her resentment of Maia? Kebi wasn't sure.

Once boarded, Maia had taken Tovyah from her and told her to stay at the back of the barque, away from Beket, Tut, and anyone else of any importance. Kebi couldn't care less if she was near the king or queen, but it wasn't fair of Maia to act like she was the one who cared for the sa nesut when she had little to do with it.

Swallowing the bit of sour bile in her mouth, Kebi held on to the side of the boat as it ferried the young couple from the palace on the western side of the Nile to the temples on the eastern shore. King Tut sat in a golden chair under an enormous canopy, Queen Ankhesenamun at his side. Even though they were siblings, they did truly seem to love each other. How much of that was due to the fact that they had been thrown into power while still children? Lost everything but each other? Did they cling to one another to protect themselves from the shifty vizier, Ay?

Ahead of them was an enormous boat, a line of men on each side as they rowed east. Oars hit the water in perfect rhythm, towing the king's barque and propelling them toward the eastern bank of the Nile.

When the vessel had crossed the mighty river, expert oarsmen steered the vessel east into an alleyway of water, bringing them to within a short walk of the massive temple complex.

A ramp was quickly shoved against the boat, and the king and his queen debarked. Once all had come ashore, a procession formed. Though this was the first time in over twenty years—since Tut's grandfather made this same journey—this particular feast had been celebrated, everyone but Kebi seemed to know exactly what to do. Her eyes darted around as she tried to figure where she belonged in the long line of people. Surely, as a mere servant, she would be in the back.

The royal couple, followed by Princess Beketaten, Vizier Ay, and the priests, paraded along a broad avenue. Ecstatic residents of Waset cheered as they passed. Huge stone ram-headed sphinxes lined both sides of the walk, ending at the entrance to the temple.

Kebi craned her neck to take in the massive gateway that seemed to reach the clouds themselves.

Beyond the gates lay an open-air courtyard. She resisted spinning as she walked, trying to take in the enormity of a temple complex that dwarfed the palace.

Tut, Ankhe, and the priests climbed the steps. Commoners, like her, could go no farther than the Great Court.

The crowd milled around, waiting for something. But what?

"The priests have to go to the other temples in the complex to get the other two gods."

Kebi turned to see Hannah standing behind her.

"Hannah! I didn't know you were here."

"I was on the other barque, with the king's and queen's attendants."

"Oh. Did anyone else from the princess's palace come?"

"Only Neferet. She came to wait on the princess, and I am to help Neferet. You and Neferet will be staying near the princess, but I will be with the queen's servants." She sounded a little bitter. Or maybe she was just tired. Kebi certainly was, though the day was not half over.

"And what are we waiting for again?"

"There are two other temples here. One for Mut, Amun's wife, and one for Khonsu, their son. The priests have to go get them, bathe them—"

"I'm sorry. Bathe them?"

Hannah chuckled. "Yes, and dress them and put them in small, gold-covered shrines. Those shrines are then put on individual barques and brought back out here. This is the only time of year the people can see them, so it's a huge celebration."

"How do you know all this?"

"Neferet's been telling me about it. She thought it would be good for me to know about the festival before I came."

Kebi would have liked that information as well, but things like that were what she missed by going to the palace only once a week. She looked around the courtyard as thousands of residents waited breathlessly for the appearance of the gods.

At the first sign of movement inside the temple, the crowd erupted into joyous praise. Priests wearing bleached white linen robes, in sets of six, carried the small boats down the steps. Tut and Ankhe walked behind them, other priests wearing leopard skin mantles following along with large numbers of musicians, singers, and dancers. Soldiers and sacrificial animals brought up the rear as the procession headed back down the avenue of sphinxes toward the boats.

At the dock, the priests carried the small barques aboard the larger ships, while everyone else returned to the vessels they arrived in.

Multitudes of men rushed to the bank and grabbed papyrus ropes. They draped the ropes over their backs and shoulders and began hauling the boats along the shore.

Kebi shook her head. "They even make slaves tow the barques upriver? Why don't they row them?"

"Oh, no. That's a huge honor. Men pray to be chosen to do that."

Kebi eyed the boat she'd arrived in. The last thing she wanted to do was get back on. Her nausea had barely subsided.

Hannah tapped her shoulder. "We can always follow the crowd. It's not far, and we'll probably get there about the same time. They can only go as fast as the men pulling the ropes."

"Sure. Lead the way."

Anything to avoid another journey by river.

※

The walk to the southern sanctuary was crowded and noisy. The route was lined with thousands of cheering people waving fans, throwing flowers, and singing, all straining to get a glimpse of the gods who were, for most of the year, locked away in temples.

Kebi and Hannah managed to get ahead of the animals, so at least it wasn't terribly smelly. Sphinxes—some with lion's heads and some with the heads of men—lined the route.

Most of the people crowded as close to the bank as possible, with soldiers keeping them back far enough to allow the men room. Once they reached the complex, Kebi and Hannah shouldered their way into the courtyard and as close to the temple itself as possible.

King Tut and Queen Ankhe ascended the granite steps to the entrance of the temple and turned to greet the people. Since restoring the worship of the entire pantheon of gods after his father's heresy, Tut was enormously popular, and the crowd made their gratitude known.

Palace priests handed him offerings for the divine triad, which the temple priests accepted, and then Tut and Ankhe disappeared into the recesses of the temple. The crowd slowly dissipated.

"What now?" Kebi asked Hannah.

"The king and his wife must now act as substitutes for Amun and Mut, and consummate the divine marriage. If they don't, nothing will grow, order will be lost. Everything will fall apart."

Kebi scoffed.

Hannah raised her hands in mock surrender. "That's what they think, not me. They'll remain in the temple for most of the festival, and at the end, he'll come out and be crowned as king again. In the meantime, there will be food, strong beer, dancers, whatever you can think of. All provided by the king."

"No wonder it's such a popular festival."

Hannah laughed, then raised a hand and smiled at someone. "Excuse me. Redji wants me."

"Who?"

"One of the queen's handmaidens. I'll see you later." She disappeared into the crowd.

Late that night, Kebi stood in the courtyard and looked up at the stars. She looked to where the star—gone for over a year now—had been for so many terrifying nights.

Images of the day had burned into her mind.

The most powerful boy in the world chanting and praying to an idol made of gold.

Food and beer being offered to gods unable to eat or drink.

Thousands of people throwing flowers, singing, and dancing in the street.

Her heart ached as she thought about the life her son was facing. Shaddai had promised Tovyah would know the truth when it was needed, but what would he do in the meantime? Would he be here next year, or the year after, as part of Tut's family, a prince of Egypt, offering prayers to Amun?

CHAPTER FIFTEEN

❖

"When he was placed outside, Pharaoh's daughter took him and brought him up as her own son."
~ Acts 7:21 (NIV) ~

The village was quiet when Kebi stepped through the gates, Tovyah sound asleep on her shoulder. The men would be home by now, each family safely gathered inside after a long day apart. The scents of freshly baked bread and root vegetable stew reminded her how much she had missed her quiet life away from the palace over the last fifteen days.

When she stepped through the doorway, Amram brightened. The smile she had fallen in love with covered his face. He jumped up and hurried to greet her, but the children reached her first.

Amram gently lifted Tovyah from her arms, and Kebi bent to pick up Aaron, smothering his face with kisses. "I missed you so much! I think you grew even taller while I was gone. It won't be long until you are as tall as Abba."

Aaron beamed. "I get bigger!" He raised his arms into the air.

She laughed. "Yes, you will."

Kebi knelt before Miriam and pulled her into a long embrace. "My big girl. I missed you too. Were you a great help to Abba?" She glanced over at Amram, who was laying Tovyah on a sleeping mat.

Miriam nodded. "He said I was the best helper ever."

Kebi kissed both cheeks. "I'm sure you were."

Aaron and Miriam scurried back to the corner where hot stew waited.

Amram reached for her waist and pulled her close, a low moan escaping. "I'm so glad you're back. I don't think I could have endured one more day without you."

She wrapped her arms around his back, resting her hands on his shoulder blades. "I missed you too."

He grinned, his eyes bright, and brought his mouth next to her ear. "Do I get as many kisses as Aaron did?"

"Later." She laughed. "Let's eat first." She grabbed his hand and pulled him toward the firepit, taking a seat between her children. "Miriam, tell me what happened in the village while I was gone."

Miriam sat up on her knees, clearly preparing to deliver a barrage of critical information. "Banaiah asked Leah to marry him. Malachi's imma had her baby, a girl. They named her Sarah. And Matthiah called Levi a name, so Levi punched him in the nose, and now he can't come outside for eight days."

Kebi listened, fascinated, as Miriam gave her information about nearly everyone in the entire village. Kebi looked to Amram at one point, who only smiled and shrugged, his mouth full of bread.

"How could you possibly know all this?"

"I listen. And I ask questions. People tell me lots of things because I'm just a girl." She grinned. "They don't think I know anything."

"They are quite wrong, apparently."

Miriam nodded triumphantly.

After the meal, Amram took the children, including Tovyah, to the roof and settled them for the night. His soft, low, story-telling voice drifted downstairs, filling Kebi with more peace than she'd felt in days. Weeks.

Footfalls sounded behind her as she stacked the last clean bowl on the small shelf over the fire.

"What story tonight?" She spoke over her shoulder.

"The flood."

"You haven't told that one in a while."

"At least three days."

She laughed.

"Tell me more about the trip."

"Not tonight. I'm glad it's over, and I don't want to think about it for a while."

"Was it that bad?" He tipped his head toward their mats, still rolled up in the opposite corner. He unrolled his and placed it on the dirt floor.

She followed him, then spread her mat on the ground next to his. "Not really. Not that way. Maia was horrible to me and tried to act like she was Tovyah's nurse, but that was to be expected. It was more the worship." She shuddered, thoughts of drunken dancers reveling in the streets filling her mind.

"You mean the false gods?" Amram sat next to her.

"That, and the *way* they worship. Men and women doing what only husbands and wives should do, dancers wearing next to nothing, strong beer. And the thought that one day…" Her voice choked. Her mind crowded with images of her baby boy, arms raised to a golden statue, offering food and drink to a created thing, chanting ridiculous rituals.

Amram reached for her hand. "I know. But we have to trust Shaddai, ahuvati."

"I'm trying. But what he may have to go through…it breaks my heart. Couldn't Shaddai have found some other way that didn't require my sweet Tovyah to worship false gods?"

"It doesn't do any good to think like that. He is the Almighty, and I'm sure He has a reason. He is certain of more than we can even begin to wonder about."

"I suppose." She tucked her feet under her and stood. "It's already late. We should go to sleep."

He rose and reached for her hand. "Stay down here with me…for a while."

"But the children—"

"Will be all right for a while. Stay with me." He let go of her hand.

It was her decision.

She laid her head on his chest. "I love you."

He kissed her temple. "I love you too. I missed you."

She raised her head to study his face. He was still as handsome as the day she met him. The dimple in his right cheek deepened as he smiled down on her. Such a gift El Shaddai had given her when she married Amram. At her age, she could have expected to be alone for the rest of her life. Instead, she had him.

He bent his head and touched his lips to hers. Warmth spread throughout her body, banishing the worries and fears, silencing her overthinking mind, and filling her with the security she always felt in his arms.

Times like this, even Maia couldn't ruin.

◆

After a too-short night, Kebi stepped through Beket's double doors, Tovyah on her hip. Last night's late arrival coupled with rising early to grind the barley had left little time for sleep.

She'd taken only a few steps before Beket bolted toward her.

"Habibi! Come here." She reached for Tovyah.

Kebi's heart panged as her son, after spending all day for two weeks with Beket, went willingly into another's arms.

"Come. I have a new food for you." She hurried toward the couches, leaving Kebi alone in the hallway.

Kebi watched the princess stroll away with her son, the hole in her heart growing bigger. She followed, pasting on a smile when Beket looked up.

The princess sat on a wide chair, her arm around Tovyah's waist as he stood next to her.

Neferet handed Beket a slice of cut fruit.

"Try this, Mose." The princess held out a slice of a soft purple fruit, and he poked at it with one chubby finger. Beket giggled. "Try it. It's good." She took a bite herself and then offered it again to Tovyah.

He bent his head to take a bite. "Mmm." He nodded and bent toward the fruit again.

Beket placed it in his hand instead and glanced at Kebi, still standing. She gestured toward a nearby couch. "Would you like one? It's a plum." She turned to her attendant. "Neferet?"

Neferet extended a platter toward her.

Kebi chose a small piece and bit off a fragment. The juice filled her mouth, and she understood the smile on Tovyah's face. Fruit this fresh was a rarity in the village. They might get their hands on some dried grapes or other dried fruit but almost never fresh off the tree.

Of course, the king and his family ate anything they could dream of. Meat, fruit, soft wheat bread, while the farmers and peasants subsisted on coarse barley bread and boiled papyrus root.

Beket grasped Tovyah by the torso and lifted him above her head. "I missed you last night."

Tovyah laughed, and she set him on his feet again.

"Shouldn't he be talking by now? The other children in the palace his age are speaking."

Kebi herself was slightly worried, but she didn't want to alarm Beket yet. What would she do if she found out her sa nesut wasn't perfect?

Hope flashed in Kebi's mind. Would she give him back? Find a perfect child?

Fear quickly replaced hope. Beket could just as easily have him destroyed.

"He's a little behind, but every baby is different."

Beket tickled his tummy. "Then we will be patient."

Tovyah giggled.

Beket cleared her throat. "Jochebed, I've been thinking."

"Yes, nebet-i?"

"After seeing Mose every day, seeing him every tenth day just isn't enough for me anymore."

What did she mean? What would be "enough"? "I could bring him more often, I suppose."

Beket stood, her tall, slender figure in silhouette against the morning sun. "That's not really what I meant. I want to see him every day."

Bringing him every day would require a great deal of work, but if that's what she had to do, she would do it. "Then I shall bring him every day, if that is what you require."

The princess stepped away. "No. I want him to live here, in the palace, with me from now on."

Kebi's breath caught. Blood pounded in her ears. Had the end finally come?

Her chest burned. "Of course, nebet-i." She swallowed past a lump in her throat. "May I say goodbye before I leave?"

"Leave? Why would you leave?" Beket spun to face her.

Had she misunderstood? "I assume you will need me no longer."

"Need you? Of course we need you. Mose adores you. I'd like you to come and nurse him each day, if you can. You've said he sleeps through the night now, so he may as well sleep here. It will be less disruptive to him if he is not carried back and forth every day."

"Of course."

"You could move here to be with him, if that's easier, but I know you have other children."

Kebi shook her head. "I couldn't leave them for good. It was hard enough during the festival."

"Then it's settled. Mahu will pick you up each morning and return you after Mose has been fed for the last time each day." She returned to her seat and reached for a piece of fruit.

How could she know she had just upended Kebi's world?

❖

If only Kebi could somehow avoid telling Amram. This would be even worse than telling him she would be gone for the festival.

This would mean nearly two years of spending every day at the palace. For Amram, it would not make much difference. She would leave each day at about the same time he did, and Beket had promised to return her before dark.

But what about Miriam and Aaron? Was it fair to ignore them for two years, just so she could have that time with Mose?

Kebi kept her secret until after the evening meal. Afterward, she kissed Miriam and Aaron good night and left them to sleep under the stars, then stepped back down to the room below. Amram had hooked the bottom edge of the reed mat to the wall above the doorway, and a slight but warm breeze skittered through the door and out the other side of the house.

He turned at the sound of her footsteps. "I know you have something to tell me."

How well he knew her. Just as well as she knew him.

She repeated the conversation she'd had that afternoon with Beket.

"You'll have to take him every day?"

She grimaced. "No…he'll live there."

Sadness filled his eyes. "So it's done? We'll never see him again after tonight?" He turned away. "We knew this would happen, but I thought we'd have more time."

"She wants me to continue to nurse him."

"What? How is that possible?"

"I would go to the palace every day."

"Every day?" He huffed. "It was bad enough when you went to the festival. How do we manage without you? You can't expect Shiphrah to take care of her family and yours for another two years."

"The princess said I could come later and leave earlier. He's not feeding as often now."

He shook his head. "I don't know."

"If I don't, we'll never see him again."

Amram's face darkened for one of the few times since she'd known him. "You mean *you'll* never see him again. I won't, either way. Nor will Miriam or Aaron." He stomped toward the door.

"Wait." Kebi followed. "Do you want me to tell her no?"

"Could you?" Hand on the doorpost, he turned and raised a brow. "Would you?"

Her heart sank to the dirt floor of their little house.

Amram shrugged. "I don't know what to think. Let me talk to El Shaddai about this." He left, his footfalls becoming softer as he marched down the village road.

Kebi put away the dishes, then sat outside, leaning against the bundle of reeds that formed the doorpost, waiting for Amram to return. The moon kept guard over her, its fullness lighting up the narrow road of their village.

The air had finally lost its oppressive swelter, and under different circumstances, the night would be enjoyable.

Inside, baby Tovyah slept, blissfully unaware of the upset his sweet life caused each day.

She recognized Amram's long strides before she could see his features. He no longer seemed to be stomping. He must have calmed.

He sat next to her, his legs stretched out in front of him, crossed at the ankles. He leaned back against the opposite post and rested his head against the wall. A soft sigh escaped him.

"Do you want me to tell her no? She said it was my choice."

"No. The longer you stay with him, the more of El Shaddai you can pour into his heart."

"Do you really think he understands anything I say?"

He shrugged. "Probably not. But Shaddai assured me he will remember it when it is time."

"Time for what?"

"Time for him to do as Shaddai asks. Time to free us from Egypt's hateful bondage."

"I'm sorry. Perhaps I should have said no at the beginning. Said goodbye at the river. Then we wouldn't be discussing this now."

"No." A slow smile spread over his face. "I've enjoyed seeing him this last year. It was a wonderful gift Shaddai didn't have to give us." He ran a calloused hand down his face. "This is a difficult time, but we'll get through it. And when it's over, we'll miss it. Heartache and all." He reached for her hand.

"Do you mean that?"

"Of course, or I wouldn't have said it."

"Sometimes it's hard for me to see that side of it. All I can think of is his being gone someday. I try to stuff a lifetime's worth of experiences into every moment he's with me."

"I know. But you have to trust Shaddai. Relax. Enjoy what moments you are given. Leave the rest to Him."

"I'll try." She meant it. But every time she left the rest to Shaddai, things seemed to get worse.

CHAPTER SIXTEEN

✧

When the child grew older, she took him to Pharaoh's daughter and he became her son.
~ Exodus 2:10 (NIV) ~

KAHORKA, FOURTH MONTH OF AKHET,
THE SEASON OF INUNDATION

Kebi's eyes shot open to find their home drenched in sunlight. How late had she slept? Amram had left for the fields already. Why hadn't he awakened her? She dragged herself to her feet, splashed water on her face, and grabbed a head scarf on her way out the door. No time to grind grain. Her family would have to do without bread today.

She bolted through the village, trying to ignore the thoughts of what Beket would say.

Mahu awaited next to the chariot, his usual calm demeanor and warm smile in place.

She climbed onto the platform, and Mahu hopped up behind her.

"How much trouble am I in?"

"I wouldn't worry too much. Beket can be very understanding." He spoke to the horses, urging them to go faster. "Do you have a good reason?"

"Are you going to tell her?"

He grinned. "Not if you don't want me to."

"I don't get much sleep. I get up before the sun to grind our grain so my daughter can make bread. It takes almost half the night."

"I see."

"What do you see?"

"I see that you are caught between two worlds."

How could he know that? How did he get it so right, when she couldn't make Amram understand?

"How…?"

"I've spent my life watching others, knowing what they are thinking and what they might do. In the army I did it to stay alive. As a Medjay, I did it to survive in another sense. When I was chief Medjay, I was often the bridge between several people, or groups of people, both Egyptian and foreign. I'm very good." He grinned at her.

"I can't even get my own husband to understand," she muttered.

"He has his own grief to deal with, does he not?"

Kebi felt all the air leave her lungs. When had she become so selfish? Amram had lost his son, for good. As difficult as it was, she saw Tovyah every day, held him close, nourished him from her own body.

Amram would never see him again.

Shaddai, forgive me.

Later that morning, after Tovyah had gone to sleep, Kebi stood before Beket, fear snaking around her heart.

"So you stay up half the night and then come here?" Beket seemed incredulous.

The woman had no idea what it took to keep a house running smoothly.

Kebi nodded.

Beket's cheeks colored the smallest bit. "I'm so sorry. I didn't even think. My attendants—they all live here. They have no other concerns to divide their attention." She frowned.

Was she thinking, or was she disappointed?

"Well, we can't have you exhausted." She shrugged. "But I can't lose you either." She paced a moment. "If I give you grain that has already been ground, would that help?"

Kebi was speechless for a moment. "Enormously, nebit-i."

"Excellent."

Mahu was right. The princess was understanding. *Thank You, Shaddai.*

And El Shaddai was good.

◆

Kebi sighed. Maia was scolding her. Again. What had she done now?

It seemed no matter what she did, it wasn't right. Kebi fed him the wrong foods, nursed him too often or too little, coddled him when she should be strict. Whatever she did, Maia found fault and was quick to make her opinion known.

But this time was different. Hannah had specifically told her Maia said he wouldn't have to have his hair cut. Now she was being chastised for not taking him to the royal barber to have his hair shaved into a sidelock, the traditional style of Egyptian children.

Maia glowered. "And why would I say that? What possible reason would I have for not allowing the sa nesut to look like the royal child he is?"

"I have no idea. I have given up trying to understand. Now I just try to obey. Would you like me to take him to the barber now?"

Maia took a quick step back. "You would do that?"

"Of course. As I said, I'm trying very hard to obey. Sometimes the words are confusing, but I try to do as you and as the princess ask."

"You are not refusing?"

Why would she think that? Had Kebi appeared obstinate, disobedient? "I am very sorry if I have made your job harder. I do not always agree with how things are done here, simply because we have different ways. But other than praying to false gods or teaching Mose to do the same, I have never intentionally disobeyed you. I am happy to have his hair cut."

"Then yes, please do."

Kebi bent over the bed and helped Tovyah to the floor.

"Kebi?"

"Yes, Maia."

"I know it's..." She seemed to be searching for the right words as her eyes glazed over, as if she were seeing into the past. "It's difficult to nurse another child as your own. To be reminded every day that he *could* be your own, if circumstances were just a little different. When you hold him close, and he drinks the life-giving milk from your own body..." She blinked and appeared to return to the present. "You must guard your heart."

Maia had no idea how right she was.

"Thank you, Maia. I'll try." She took Tovyah by the hand. "Can you tell me where in the palace the barber is?"

"You don't know? Hannah didn't tell you?"

"No, was she supposed to?"

"Go across the walkway to the main palace. Ask the doorkeeper to take you."

Kebi smiled as brightly as possible before she headed toward the double doors that led to the walkway to the king's palace. Anything to keep from being labeled disobedient. Argumentative. A problem.

At another set of double doors, she paused while the doorkeeper allowed her in. "Can you show me to the royal barber?"

"Of course, but you must be escorted. Please follow me."

The guard led them into the king's receiving hall. The floor was painted with a scene of birds in a marsh, the king hunting them. Successfully, apparently, judging by the pile of dead birds at his feet. Enormous columns—twelve on each side—rose on either side of her, several strides apart. Brightly painted, they ended in stone pomegranates at the top.

At the end of the room he turned right into a narrow hallway, then halted abruptly.

Kebi peered around the guard's broad shoulder to see Mahu's smiling face.

"I'll take them from here. You may return to your post."

The doorkeeper saluted and disappeared.

"Mahu. Em hotep." She bowed her head.

He chuckled. "Your words are correct, but your accent is atrocious."

"As always, I'm sure."

"Usually it's not too bad." He turned around and led her farther into the palace of Tutankhamun. Kebi bent to scoop up Tovyah so they could keep pace.

Mahu spoke over his shoulder. "The barber, tailor, and other craftsmen who serve the king are in the next building."

She glanced at the rows of rooms on either side of another elaborate hall as they turned left. "Does the queen live in one of these?"

"Ankhesenamun's rooms are in the north palace with her attendants, though she spends a great deal of time with the king and more often than not sleeps in his room." He led her out of the main palace, across an open area, and into another building. When they stepped inside, Kebi set Tovyah on his feet.

"The barber's room is here." Mahu extended an arm.

Kebi moved toward the open door, but Tovyah planted his feet firmly on the tile floor, pulling on her hand.

He shook his head violently, little eyes wide with fright.

Kebi glanced at the guard, who seemed to be at a loss as to what to do. "This is why we don't cut their hair until they are three," she said.

He smirked. "This is why we start when they are infants."

She laughed. "I guess we're a little late."

"Is this your idea or Beket's?"

"Certainly not mine." She frowned. "Maia's. Hannah told me Maia said he didn't have to shave his head, but then Maia scolded me for not having done it already. I don't know how to please that woman. Everything I do seems to disappoint her."

Mahu raised a brow.

Her hand went to her mouth. "I'm so sorry. That was terribly disrespectful. Please forgive me."

"Of course." One corner of his mouth turned up. "I have an idea." He knelt to look the prince in the eye. "If I have my head shaved first, will you do it next?"

Tovyah grinned and bobbed his head.

"Come then." Mahu rose and took Tovyah by the hand and led him into the room. He approached the barber. "Pentu, I would like a fresh shave."

"Yes, Captain. Please sit."

Mahu beckoned to Tovyah. "Mose, come here. Why don't you stand here so you can watch everything the man is doing?" He wrapped his long hands around Tovyah's torso and lifted him onto the nearby stool. Then Mahu sat on the stool the barber gestured to.

Pentu picked up a bronze blade set into a wooden handle.

Kebi moved behind Tovyah and laid a hand on his back.

The barber applied a frothy cream to Mahu's head, then skimmed the straight edge over it in long strokes. When he finished, he rubbed a cloth over Mahu's head, and pulled it away covered in short gray hairs and cream.

Mahu raised one hand, palm up. "See? Doesn't hurt. Now your turn. I'll stay right here, and you can either stand up or sit down."

Tovyah needed no more encouragement, and raised his arms so Mahu could lift him onto the barber's stool, then extended a hand to the captain.

Mahu wrapped his hand around the much smaller one and held it tight while the craftsman shaved all but an area about the size of a child's fist on the left side of Tovyah's head. He set the blade aside, then deftly braided the remaining hair and tied the bottom with a length of papyrus reed.

Pentu stepped back. "Finished."

Mahu thanked the man, then turned to Tovyah. "Not too bad, huh?" Mahu asked.

Tovyah nodded, a huge smile on his face.

"Thank you," Kebi said to Mahu. "You saved me from a sure tongue-lashing."

Mahu chuckled. "I've been on the wrong end of those."

"I'm sure we can find our way back. Thank you for your help."

"I still need to escort you."

Kebi took her son's hand as they returned to Beket's palace, Mahu following silently behind.

The princess waited in the receiving room. Her face lit up when she saw Tovyah. "There is my little sa nesut. You look very Egyptian now."

It was true. He looked more like Beket's son, like a prince of Egypt.

Slowly but surely, Kebi was losing him.

He was no longer Tovyah.

He was Mose.

◆

Kebi stood at the edge of the portico, leaning against a column, as Mose played with a stuffed leather ball in the courtyard. The sun crept toward the west, and the heavy, unmoving air had cooled a bit.

Miu sauntered into the yard. Mose had come to adore her, and for some reason, the cat put up with all the poking and prodding a toddler could inflict on a living toy.

Mose plopped to the ground, and the cat climbed into his lap. He laughed as she licked his arms and rubbed her head against his.

Kebi cringed at the thought of cat saliva on her skin.

Miu began to groom herself, Mose interfering, and at some point, apparently decided she had had enough and bolted from his lap.

Mose scrambled to his feet and chased after her. He had almost caught up when his chubby feet tangled in each other and he fell, skidding on his belly in the hot, hard-packed earth. He sat up and looked at his hands.

She could see the blood droplets from where she stood. Not bad but enough to sting. She stepped closer. If she seemed too concerned, he would cry, so she calmed her face. "You're all right."

He stood and ran toward her. *"Muu! Muu!"*

Her heart leaped. His first words. Just when she was becoming seriously worried. And like most children, his first word was a child's version of *mother.*

She hurried toward him, her arms out—and he ran right past her.

To Beket. When had she returned from her bath?

Horror descended on her like a moonless night. She slowly spun toward them.

"Muu!" He showed her his hands, and Beket kissed his cuts. Kissed his cheeks. Swallowed him in a long embrace.

The moment they had both been waiting for had finally happened. And it was not Kebi's to savor.

Beket turned his hands palms up and wiped away the tiny crimson droplets. "Shhh. It's all right. All better now, see?"

Kebi disappeared inside. She hurried across the open area and into Mose's room. She closed the door and fell against it, her heart racing, her chest heaving.

His words had pierced her soul as surely as a blade. Her throat constricted, and hot tears flooded her face.

The sound every mother lives for, celebrates, and treasures in her heart was not meant for her.

Couldn't Shaddai have given her one time, just once, to hear him call her *imma,* before Beket stole his heart?

Footsteps on the tiled floor outside warned her someone approached. She rushed to the bowl of water on the chest near his bed and quickly washed and dried her face. Hopefully her eyes weren't too red and swollen.

"Jochebed! Did you hear him?" Beket shoved open the door, her excited voice preceding her entry into the room, Mose in her arms.

Kebi stepped away from the bed and forced a smile. "Yes, I heard him. You must be thrilled."

Beket sniffled, cupping his cheek. "I thought I would never have children. There was no one my father thought worthy of marriage to me, and then once we came here... I'd given up that dream long ago." Tears filled her eyes.

Happy tears.

How could one small word fill one woman with delirious joy and consume another with agonizing grief?

CHAPTER SEVENTEEN

❖

*But you, Lord, are a shield around me, my glory,
the One who lifts my head high.*
~ Psalm 3:3 (NIV) ~

The chariot rumbled along the raised path from the palace complex to the village.

Kebi tried to make sure she didn't look as agonized as she felt. She couldn't have Mahu see her crying. It would eventually get back to Maia, and they would both figure out that Mose was her own son.

She managed to arrive at the village gate without giving herself away. She hoped.

Mahu held out his hand to help her down. "Did something happen at the palace today? Was Maia too harsh again?"

"No, of course not. All is well," she lied.

"I'll see you in the morning, then?"

"Of course."

Mose had been going to sleep for the night without nursing for the last week or more. Kebi had been staying until he lay down, but today she left after she fed him last, before their evening meal was served. When she arrived at the house, she sent Miriam outside and prepared her family's food.

Kebi kept silent all through their evening meal, afraid to speak lest the words never stop tumbling out. Miriam and Aaron had both asked her why she was sad. She lied and said she was merely tired. They seemed to believe her.

Amram didn't.

The last morsels gone and everything washed and put away, she went to sit beside Amram, who had been patiently waiting for her to tell him what had happened.

"He called her imma today. Well, he didn't say it quite right. He said 'muu.' *Muut* is Egyptian for mother."

"I'm sorry." Amram put his arm around her shoulder.

"He ran right past me, to *her*. It hurt so much I thought I would die." The memory burned fresh all over again.

"Did it hurt more than when you put him in the river?"

It hadn't, really. Thinking she would never hold him, never raise him, never know what happened to him was far worse.

"You knew this was bound to happen," Amram said.

She did know, had always known, but it didn't lessen the ache. At all. "But hearing it… I just wasn't prepared for it. It felt like complete and total rejection."

"He doesn't know you are his imma. It's not rejection. He is doing what he should be doing. Would you rather he spent his life hating her for taking him from you?"

"No, I suppose not."

"And, you must remember, she did not take him from you. Shaddai did. If she did anything, she saved his life. No matter what, he cannot stay here. It sounds like she is a very good option."

He was right, she knew.

If only her mind could convince her heart.

◆

Kebi laughed until her sides hurt. Amram once again placed his lips on Aaron's belly and blew. The child squirmed and laughed, his hands on his abba's cheeks.

The day Beket had allowed her to spend in the village had been like balm to her soul.

She looked at the starry sky, frowning.

When had it gotten so dark? The day had flown by.

"I think you two need to go up and go to sleep."

"Do we have to?"

"Don't whine, Aaron. If you wake up in time, I'll see you in the morning."

"Yes, Imma." Miriam dutifully stood and held her hand out to Aaron. "Come on, brother."

Aaron took his big sister's hand and followed her up the stairs.

Kebi gathered the bowls and stood to take them to the corner cistern so she could wash them before getting a good night's sleep for once. She hummed. Amram's soft smile, Miriam's curls, Aaron's giggle—they filled a hole in her heart she hadn't realized existed.

Miriam had learned to make quite good bread, as long as she had ground flour. She had loved showing Kebi all the tasks she had learned to perform while Kebi was away each day.

Aaron, who had somehow seemed to grow a head taller in the three months since the festival, didn't need much persuasion to stay home with her. He'd grown quite comfortable playing with Shiphrah's boys next door, but a day with Imma was still better than roughhousing.

For the last three months she'd spent all day, every day at the palace, caring for Mose, telling him stories of their ancestors and El Shaddai, filling his ears with tales that showed the Almighty's love for him and his people. Someday, as Shaddai promised, Mose would remember who his people were, and he would know their stories.

He would know he was not Egyptian but one of their slaves. Not one of the rulers but one of the oppressed.

She had no idea when or how that would happen, but she could imagine how hard that day would be for him. She prayed it would not destroy him but fill him with a new passion.

El Shaddai, keep him safe. Guard his heart. I cannot do it—it must be You.

◆

With dawn's faint fingers reaching through the window, Kebi rose and dressed in the dark. Her breasts ached to feed Mose, and her heart ached to see him.

Aaron's little feet appeared on the top steps. Why was he up so early? He continued his climb down, rubbing his eyes when he at last reached the floor.

"Motek, why are you awake? You should go back to bed. Even Abba is not awake yet."

"Are you leaving already?" The sorrow in his eyes nearly broke her heart.

"Yes, Aaron. I have to go back to baby Tovyah. He is hungry, and I have to feed him."

"Stay one more day?" His voice wavered, and her heart skipped a beat knowing she had caused his pain.

"I'm sorry, but I can't."

"I miss you when you're gone." He reached his arms up.

She picked him up, and he wrapped his arms around her neck and his feet around her waist, clinging to her as if he could keep her here just by wishing hard enough.

She returned his fierce embrace. "I miss you too," she whispered.

"Then why can't you stay with us?"

"Have you forgotten Tovyah already?" He'd been living in the palace only a few months, but it felt as if he had never lived here. She glanced around. She'd given away the clothes that would no longer fit him even if he were here. There were no toys, no sandals—not a single reminder of him.

"No, I don't forget him, but he has a princess to take care of him now." He spoke into her neck. "And we have no one." He squeezed even harder.

His words were like a knife through her heart.

"Aaron, motek. Look at me."

He raised his head and met her gaze with an earnest openness.

"You still have me. I won't be able to take care of Tovyah much longer, because you're right, the princess takes care of him. But I have to stay with him as long as I can and teach him about El Shaddai because once I leave, no one else will ever teach him about the living God. Do you understand?"

He nodded. "Yes. But I still miss you."

"I miss you too. But I love you, and I will never leave you. So I need you to be patient, because soon I will have to leave your brother."

"Yes, Imma."

He placed a sloppy kiss on her mouth and hugged her one last time before she set him down.

Her heart ached as she walked down the road toward the chariot. It ripped her heart out every morning when she left for the palace.

How much longer could she endure this?

◆

That evening, Kebi stepped through the doorway, then halted as if she'd run into a wall.

A large pottery bowl of stew held in both hands, Miriam leaned to the side to calm down Aaron. "It's almost ready, motek. You don't need to cry." She took the stew to the roof.

Aaron sniffled, a few stray teardrops on his pink cheeks, then dropped to the floor in a heap. He did have on a clean tunic, and his hair had been brushed. Amram was doing as much as he could while she spent the day in a palace.

Kebi crossed the small room in three strides and scooped up the crying boy.

"Imma!" He wrapped his arms around her neck and squeezed as if he hadn't seen her in a month.

"I'm sorry, motek. I'm sorry I have to be gone all day," she whispered.

"It's all right. I understand. Baby Tovyah needs you too."

She brushed the hair from his face. "Abba brushed your hair today?"

He shook his head.

"You did it by yourself?"

"No. Miriam." He shot out an arm and pointed to Miriam carrying a loaf of hot bread.

"And she washed my tunic in the river for me." He dropped his gaze. "I got mud all over it. I'm sorry."

"It's all right. You're allowed to get dirty." He'd be making bricks soon enough. Might as well enjoy playing in the dirt while he could.

He squirmed out of her arms and onto the floor. "I help." He ran to Miriam, who gave him the basket of bread to carry upstairs.

Amazement filled Kebi as she watched Miriam prepare the evening meal. She glanced around the house. Sandals neatly lined up by the door, Aaron's toys in a basket in the corner. Clean tunics folded and placed on the single shelf.

Her only daughter taking over tasks she shouldn't have to do yet.

Kebi took a jug of beer from Miriam and followed her upstairs. "Did you do all this by yourself?"

Miriam shrugged. "Yes. It wasn't so hard. Nathanael's imma helped me with the washing."

Kebi's cheeks heated. "I'll have to tell her thank you." She should be the one teaching Miriam these things.

Two of her children in one house, a third in another. Her heart broke in two. They should all be together. It wasn't natural, this situation of theirs.

Her exhaustion, Aaron's tears, Miriam growing up too fast. Had Kebi paid too high a price to remain with Mose?

◆

This was not the way being a mother was supposed to feel. A mother should never have to choose between her children, yet she was forced to place one over the others every day.

Mahu smiled as she neared the vehicle. "Em hotep, Kebi."

"Good morning to you." She accepted his hand and climbed into the chariot.

The horses began to trot west without his command.

"Your words say good morning, but your face says otherwise." Mahu looked straight ahead as he spoke.

"I'm sorry. I do not mean to weigh you down with my small troubles."

"How long have I been taking you to and from the palace?"

She didn't need to count the days. Every one was burned into her memory. "Over a year."

"Yes. Have I ever once betrayed your confidence, given you cause to mistrust me?"

She furrowed her brow. "Of course not." What was he trying to say?

"Then can we not be considered friends?"

She stared at the floor of the chariot. "You are Egyptian, the highest of the Medjay. I am but a slave. I cannot be your friend."

"I disagree. We have pleasant conversation. We trust one another. I would never allow harm to come to you, and I have no doubt you would do whatever you could to help me if needed. What more do we need to be friends?"

He had a point. There were women in the village she could not say the same about, would not consider friends. "I suppose you're right."

The horses curved to the north along the causeway toward the palace complex.

"Then why does sadness haunt your face this morning?"

"I hate saying goodbye to my...children each morning." She caught herself before saying *other children*. What questions would that have brought up?

"I'm sorry. I know that must be painful. And knowing that you will soon be with them again every day probably doesn't help."

The thought of saying a final goodbye nearly made her sick.

He drew in a deep breath. "Do you remember when I came to your house, when the long-tailed star was still in the sky?"

Her breath caught. He knew. He had never said anything, but *he knew.*

"We lost our only child."

Had she heard him correctly? His voice had become so soft it was hard to tell. "What?"

"We lost our only child. Maia and I. Many years ago now, but the ache never leaves completely. I think that was why I couldn't bring myself to take anyone else's child from them."

"I'm so sorry. I didn't know."

"I had just become Chief of the Medjay at Akhenaten's palace after serving in Nubia. Maia and I have known each other since we were children. We had finally married, and we were filled with joy when she became pregnant. When our daughter was born, I thought I could not possibly be any happier. We had four incredible months with her. The best time of our lives. Then she became ill." His voice broke, and he paused for a long moment.

"When our child died, Maia was asked to be the menat nesut for Beketaten. She is Akhenaten's daughter by Kiya, and Nefertiti did not want the same nurse for her children and Kiya's. At the time, it was good for her. For both of us really. It kept us distracted from thinking about her so often." He smiled, obviously remembering happier times.

"After Beket was weaned, Maia nursed several other children of the high officials. After many years, Tutankhamun was born. As the only son of Akhenaten, he was highly favored. Maia was chosen to nurse him and was named Great Royal Nurse. Once Tut was weaned, she continued to raise him and

Beketaten. She was with them more than their mother was. There were always children around us." His face darkened. "None were ours, though. With Maia constantly feeding, she was never able to become with child again. We contented ourselves with Akhenaten's children."

"Mahu, I'm so sorry."

"So I know what you are feeling."

"Thank you," she whispered.

He returned his attention to the road before them. "Tut may be the king, but Maia can still instill fear in him." He laughed.

The gate opened, and they entered the complex. Mahu drove her to Beketaten's door. When he stepped down to offer her a hand, he leaned in. "If you tell anyone what I have said about Tut, I will deny it, and we can no longer be friends."

From anyone else that would have sounded like a threat. But from Mahu, it was more like a confession.

"I would never do that to a friend."

His smile warmed her. "I'll see you at dusk."

Maia was certainly dour, but what if Kebi had never known the blessing of children? Barrenness was considered a curse. Would such a curse have turned Kebi into a sour, bitter old woman like Maia?

Perhaps she could be a little more undersanding of Maia from now on.

CHAPTER EIGHTEEN

*"For I know the plans I have for you," declares the L*ORD*, "plans to prosper you and not to harm you, plans to give you hope and a future."*
~ Jeremiah 29:11 (NIV) ~

TA-AABET, FIRST MONTH OF PERET, THE SEASON OF GROWING

The nursing session over, Kebi allowed Beket to take the sleepy, satisfied toddler from her.

"Isn't he the most beautiful child you have ever seen?" Beket beamed at him. "How could anyone give you away?"

Kebi's stomach somersaulted. *If only you knew.* She dropped her gaze and studied her fingernails. If she kept watching him in another's arms, she would give herself away.

"Actually, I think it must have been very hard for his mother to place him in the water, don't you?"

How did Kebi respond to that?

"I think she must have loved you very much to do what she did." Beket's voice was soft. "To allow another to raise you, to love you, to see you grow into a man, rather than let the Medjay hurt you... I think that is the bravest thing anyone could ever do." She stroked his cheek.

A burning pain started in Kebi's heart, spreading through her chest, up her throat....*Don't cry.*

"Princess Beketaten!" The voice reverberated off the tiled walls.

Beket's face paled, and she shoved Mose toward Kebi. She pressed her shoulders back, sucked in a breath, and marched out to the receiving hall.

Kebi waited until Beket was well clear of the doorway before peering around the door.

A Medjay stood as straight as one of the pillars lining the hallway, his face expressionless. "The *hemet nesut* would like to visit you."

The Royal Wife? Ankhesenamun had spent the entire festival avoiding both Beket and the sa nesut. Why would she show up now?

Kebi's shoulders relaxed slightly.

"Of course. She is more than welcome. You may bring her here at any time."

The guard nodded to another at the door to the hall. He pulled on the door, revealing the wife of Tutankhamun. The jewelry adorning her arms, wrists, neck, ankles—if sold—would feed Kebi's village for years. The kohl on her eyelids extended halfway to her ears. Barely halfway through her teen years, her face still boasted the rounded cheeks of a child.

And yet she was somehow different from how she appeared across the river.

Kebi studied the young queen. Clothes, hair—wig—makeup, all seemed unchanged.

Then it hit her. A bright smile lit her face in a way Kebi had never seen before.

What was the cause of her happiness?

As Ankhe had entered, servants had rushed to arrange two wide-seated armchairs and a low table. Platters of sliced fruit and nuts and pitchers of wine were set on the table.

"Ankhesenamun, King's Daughter of his Body, beloved of Tutankhamun, King of Upper and Lower Egypt, Son of Ra, Living Image of Amun, I am honored at your presence." Beket bowed deeply.

Ankhe stepped near and touched Beket on the shoulder. "Please rise." Her voice was soft.

Beket stood, but she kept her eyes down.

"Beketamun, I would like to talk to you."

"Of course. Would you like to enjoy some fruit and wine, or would you rather remain here?"

Ankhe gestured toward the chairs. "Let's sit."

Beket led her to the area the servants had hastily arranged, then stepped back to allow Ankhe to choose a seat first. Once Ankhe had been seated, Beket took the other chair.

"Where is your son?" Ankhe scanned the hall.

"He is in his room, with his menat. He will not bother you."

"No, I'd like to see him. Can you bring him out?"

"If you desire. I'll return in a moment."

Beket strode toward Kebi. She hurried to the couch so it wasn't obvious she'd been eavesdropping.

Beket marched through the door. "Jochebed?"

Kebi rose and headed for Beket, and when she reached her, offered Mose to her.

"Can you please join us?"

"You want me out there?" She pointed toward the hall. "You don't want to hold him?"

"It wouldn't be proper. I need to focus on the queen, so I need you to care for Mose while the queen and I speak. Just sit near us and keep him happy. And quiet." She shook her head. "I have no idea what's going on. She's avoided children and babies since..." Beket huffed and exited.

Kebi looked down at her tunic. Now she understood Beket's insistence that Kebi wear the nicer linen ones Beket had given her. Anyone could show up at any time.

Kebi followed Beket toward the circle of chairs. Another one had been added while they were in the private area.

Beket took her seat again, and Kebi sat next to her on the edge of her chair. Who would believe her if she went home and said she had sat a breath away from Tut's queen?

Ankhe watched Mose's every move. "May I hold him?"

Beket nodded to Kebi, and Kebi stood and placed the child on Ankhe's lap.

Mose stared at the new woman. He reached a hand for her bracelets, clinking them together.

"He's beautiful, Beket."

"Thank you."

Ankhe returned him to Kebi and then cleared her throat. "I've been told I've treated you quite unfairly. I came to apologize."

"No apology is necessary, I assure you."

"But it is. I would like to be your friend, Beket. I've been quite lonely since we moved here." She shifted in her seat. "I left everything I knew behind—my home, including my god, even my name."

"I know," Beket said. "I didn't leave my god, and I refuse to change my name, but I know how it hurts to abandon everything you know."

"You are the only sister I have left. They're all gone." Ankhe stared into the distance, and sadness filled her eyes.

"You want me as your sister?" Beket asked.

"You are now." Ankhe smiled. "We may not share a mother, but we are both daughters of the king."

"I would happily claim you as my sister."

"Wonderful. Now let's have some of this delicious fruit."

Kebi held Mose, feeding him bits of fruit and repeatedly picking up the wooden horse he delighted in throwing on the floor.

Ankhe and Beket chattered like lifelong friends.

It certainly seemed to make Beket happy. And Ankhe seemed to be genuine in her desire to have Beket closer.

But Kebi couldn't avoid thinking that all was not as it seemed.

◆

Kebi had just laid Mose on the bed for his afternoon nap when Beket strode into the room, her face as hard as iron.

"Come. Now." She turned around and marched back out.

Kebi placed a kiss on Mose's cheek and hurried to catch up.

Beket waited in the center of the large hall, arms folded across her chest. "You're his imma, aren't you?" Her eyes shot fire, her words were clipped.

How could she possibly know? Did she figure it out on her own, or did someone tell her? And what was Kebi supposed to say now?

Kebi studied the pattern in the tile floor. "I am."

Beket fisted her hands at her chest and released a loud, painful groan. "I should have known! Who else would do what you have done? No one would leave her family every day to come here to nurse another woman's child. How could you do this to me?" She stomped away several paces, only to spin back and march straight for Kebi. "How? Why?"

Do to *her*? What had she done to her? If you asked her, the harm was done to Kebi, not Beket.

"I have done nothing to you! I have never tried to usurp your authority. I have done what you asked. I came here because you said he wouldn't suckle from anyone else. Without me, your son would be dead."

Beket stepped nearer, her face wet with tears. "You will remember who you are talking to." She continued to approach, so close that Kebi had to step backward. "I am the King's Daughter of his Body. I am the sister of King Tutankhamun, He of the Good Laws, Who Pacifies the Two Lands, He who Wears the Crowns and Satisfies the gods." She finally stopped, her finger jabbing at Kebi. "You are a slave, an Israelite, and I could snap my fingers and have you killed, right here, before my eyes for any reason or no reason at all. You have no right to speak to me in such a manner."

Kebi dropped to her knees so fast her knees hit the hard marble floor. Pain shot through her thighs as she touched her head to the floor. "Please forgive me, Princess Beketaten. Of course you are right. I am nothing in your sight, and I owe my very life to you. I humbly beg for your mercy."

Kebi stilled her body, held her breath. Silent words, however, flowed from her heart like the river during inundation.

El Shaddai, I have been selfish. I have refused to follow your instructions, and I have tried to keep Tovyah for myself. But for my sweet children, who have waited patiently for me at home while I have devoted myself to the son I have here, please save me from the wrath of this princess, which I so richly deserve.

"Stand up." Beket's voice was considerably softer but still not at all kind.

Kebi scrambled to her feet, keeping her head down.

"Look at me."

Trembling, she slowly raised her eyes. What would she see? She had never encountered anyone as angry as the princess. Not even the overseers were so angry, they were merely cruel and uncaring.

"I do not intend to have you killed. I do not even intend to have you flogged. But I cannot begin to explain how deeply you have hurt me. I obviously can't allow you to remain here as Mose's menat. Please go. Mahu is in the main palace, but another chariot is waiting for you."

That was all? No punishment, no beating, nothing?

And yet, in one way, maybe the only way that counted, banishment from her son's presence was the worst thing Beket could ever do. Kebi wasn't even being allowed to say goodbye.

"Thank you." Kebi turned to go, but paused. "I am very sorry for hurting you. That was never my intention."

A hint of forgiveness appeared on the princess's face but vanished like water drops on a hot oven.

She headed for the doors. Hannah sat in one of the waiting areas nearby, and jumped up to meet her.

"Oh, Kebi. I'm so sorry this happened! This is terrible. The princess can be so cruel." She wrapped her arms around Kebi, squeezing tightly.

"Thank you. I must go now." She pulled Hannah's arms from her neck and went to the doors.

"Goodbye," Hannah called out.

Hand on the door, Kebi looked over her shoulder.

If she didn't know better, she'd swear that there was just a hint of a smile before Hannah spun on her heel and left.

◆

Kebi couldn't stop crying. If she were Isis, surely her tears would send the waters of the Nile raging over the desert sands.

The rumble of chariot wheels drew her attention, and she looked up to see Mahu maneuvering the chariot toward the inner doors. She quickly swiped the tears from her cheeks. She'd hoped she wouldn't have to face him. He'd known Mose was her son since—when? That first day? Would he think her ridiculous for crying over something that she'd always known would happen?

Eventually. Not today. Not with no warning, no time to even kiss him goodbye.

Mahu jumped from the chariot and offered his hand, not a trace of condemnation in his eyes.

"I was expecting someone else. The princess said you were busy elsewhere."

"Maia found me and asked me to take you home." He smiled weakly. "But I can get someone else if you prefer."

"No, it's all right."

He obviously knew what had happened. No need for yet another to hear about her deception.

Kebi took his proffered hand and climbed onto the platform.

Mahu jumped up and stood beside her, then spoke softly to the horses and guided the chariot out of the palace complex and onto the raised road that led to her village.

His shoulders tightened. "I'm sorry about what happened today."

"I never wanted to hurt her."

"I know."

"Did Maia know? Before…"

He turned to meet her gaze. "I didn't tell her." He returned his attention to the road. "But she'd figured it out on her own."

"How?"

"She's either been a menat or in charge of all the menatu for most of her life. She knows how they act, how they speak to the child, how they care for a babe not their own. You were different."

"Is she angry?"

He shook his head. "No. As I said, she only wants what is best for the prince. That's all she's ever wanted, for any of the children in her care. And who better to care for Mose than his mother?"

The words stung, like salt poured on a fresh cut. "I'm not his mother. The princess is."

"You are his mother too, and always will be."

They rode in silence until they reached the village gate. Mahu faced her one last time. "And so you know, I don't think Maia was the one who told Beket. I don't know who else could have, but I truly don't think it was Maia. She asked me to tell you that she is sad to see you go."

For some reason, Kebi believed him. Her relationship with the older woman had grown more comfortable lately, though even if she stayed at the palace she would probably never be as close to her as she was to Mahu. There was simply too much pain between them.

"Thank you for being such a good friend to me this last year and a half. I'll miss you."

"I'll miss you too." He glanced toward the gate. "Now, go hug your children, and thank your God you have them."

She was beyond thankful she had Aaron and Miriam, but not even the unquestioning, overflowing love of a child could fill the gaping hole in her heart.

Kebi managed to hide her misery well enough to shoo the children outside and prepare the evening meal, giving Miriam a well-deserved break. At the sight of Amram's strong but gentle form in the doorway, however, she lost her battle.

"The princess sent me home." Her shoulders shook as words drenched in tears tumbled out.

"I can't understand a word you're saying. Are you hurt?" Keeping his hands on her upper arms, Amram stepped back, and his eyes searched her from head to toe.

Am I hurt? What a ridiculous question. She was destroyed, devastated, shattered into a million pieces that could never be put back together in quite the same way.

"Somehow the princess found out that I was Tovyah's mother. She said I had deceived her, and I couldn't stay there anymore."

Amram pursed his lips. "I see."

"You see *what*? That our son is gone? That our family is broken?" She wrenched free and stomped away.

"Our family is not broken." His voice was firm, flat. "For a reason we cannot begin to know or understand, Shaddai has chosen this way to free his people. And we were chosen"—his voice wavered—"to bring him into this world and teach him about the living God. Think about that, Jochebed."

She looked up and met his eyes.

He closed the distance between them. "We have Miriam and Aaron. And we have each other. We are not *broken*."

"I'm sorry." How many times had she said that today?

"Tovyah will always be in our hearts. We will miss him, and yes, it will hurt. But that is the plan of El Shaddai."

She nodded against his solid chest. His steady heartbeat calmed hers, and her breathing returned to normal. He rubbed her back as his words sank deep into her heart.

"I'll get some food ready."

"It's ready. Why don't you go to the roof and let us bring it to you, for once?"

That wasn't his job. It was hers. But he had offered, and she needed to quiet her heart.

She climbed the stairs. Aaron sat in the middle of the roof, alone.

"Aaron, motek, why are you up here instead of with Nathanael?"

"I saw you crying."

"What?"

"I saw you crying, so I came here to wait for you."

"But why did you wait up here?"

"So you can talk to Abba first."

How was he so wise for a boy of four years?

"My sweet boy. Come here." She sat on the floor.

Aaron hurried over and wrapped his arms around her shoulders, placing a sloppy wet kiss on both cheeks. "I'm sorry you are sad, Imma."

"I'm not any longer. I have you."

He climbed onto her lap, his back against her chest.

She wrapped her arms around him and squeezed.

"Imma, I can't breathe." Aaron giggled.

"Just one more." Laughing, she gave him a final squeeze before she released him.

He bounced to his feet. "I'll go help." He ran to the stairs, and a moment later returned carrying a large reed basket full of warm bread. Miriam came up with pottery bowls, and Amram brought up the pot of stew.

Tovyah was gone. One day, Miriam would marry and leave.

Kebi would be left with only Aaron. Eventually he would marry, and if Shaddai blessed them, he would fill their home with grandchildren.

It wasn't what she'd hoped for, what she would choose. But she would have to content herself with that.

CHAPTER NINETEEN

The Lord himself goes before you and will be with you; he will never leave you nor forsake you. Do not be afraid; do not be discouraged.
~ Deuteronomy 31:8 (NIV) ~

A child's cry broke the usual calm that settled over the village each morning after the men and older boys had departed for the brickfields. Kebi peeked out of her door to see what had caused the outburst.

Mahu strode down the street. For only a moment, her stomach tightened as she remembered the last time he had come into the village, his Medjay behind him, leaving a trail of blood.

But he was also the one who had saved her son that day.

She stepped into the street and waited for him.

His face brightened when he saw her. "Jochebed, I have come to take you to the palace."

Her blood ran cold. "Why?"

"The princess has asked for you."

Had Beketaten decided to punish her after all? Was she to be killed? "Do you know why she has sent you to get me?"

His smile faded, a bit. "No, she did not say."

"May I see to my children first?"

"I'll wait at the chariot." He turned and marched west.

"Imma?"

Miriam's voice startled her. She pasted on a smile and turned. "Yes, Miriam?"

"Why is that soldier here? Isn't he the one who takes you to the palace?"

"He's not a soldier, motek. He's a guard, and yes, that's Mahu. I have to go see the princess. I'm sure I won't be gone long. Keep an eye on Aaron for me, all right?"

"Yes, Imma." She ran toward Kebi and grabbed her legs. "I love you, Imma."

Kebi lowered herself to kneel before her daughter. "What's that about?"

"What if you don't come back?"

"Why would you think that? I've come back every other time."

"I know she's angry with you."

"I think if she were going to hurt me she would have done it then, don't you?" Who exactly was she trying to convince, Miriam, or herself?

Miriam nodded, a smile fighting to show itself.

"Then don't worry, say a prayer to El Shaddai, and I'll be back soon." She kissed her daughter's head and marched toward the chariot.

She should give the same advice to herself.

❖

"Jochebed, thank you for coming." Beket turned to her handmaiden. "Some refreshments, please."

Neferet bowed and disappeared.

"Your word is law, nebet-i. I am ashamed of my actions and once again beg your mercy." Kebi bowed her head.

"We need to talk about the other day. Please sit with me." She led Kebi to the courtyard's portico.

Neferet appeared, setting a platter of sliced fruit and a pitcher of juice on the low table beside them. She poured two goblets before leaving.

"Kebi—that's what you are called, is it not?"

"Yes, nebet-i."

"Kebi, look at me." Her voice was soft, almost a whisper.

Kebi met the princess's gaze.

"I am the one who is sorry. I should never have sent you away. I was hurt, scared, and angry, and I took it out on you."

"But I was the one who hurt you."

"Perhaps, but I'm sure it was unintentional. Could you really have told me the day I hired you that Mose was your own son?"

You tell me.

"I understand why you did what you did. After you left—after I sent you away, I thought about what it would feel like to lose Mose. I can't even imagine life without him now, and he's only been with me daily for two months. What you must have felt when you had to leave him here for the first time—I'm sorry."

"It...it was..." How did she put into words the absolute agony of that day? "It was devastating, yes. But my son was alive. Others weren't."

Realization brightened Beket's face. "Ah, now I understand what you meant when you said your position in the village was—how did you put it—precarious. And why Amram was beaten."

Kebi shuddered, remembering the blood that covered Amram's back.

"Is it any better?"

"Yes, it is."

"Kebi." Beket set her golden goblet aside. "Mose hasn't stopped asking for you since you left."

Kebi's heart leaped. "He hasn't?"

"He loves you, you know."

The dam broke, and tears rushed down her cheeks.

The princess rose and hurried to Kebi's side. She bent down and wrapped her arms around her. "I love you too. Mose needs both of us right now. I'd like you to come back. We need to do this together. But we need to figure out how to do that."

"I will do whatever you ask, nebet-i."

Beket pulled her chair closer and perched on the edge. "I saw your face the day he called me muut."

"Is that how you knew?"

"No... someone told me. But then I remembered your reaction that day, and a few other times as well. It explained a lot." She picked at her fingernails. "But I think maybe...I always knew. When I heard that, it explained a lot of things I had wondered about."

"*You* are his mother now." As much as it hurt to admit that, Kebi knew it was true.

"As are you. But you know no one else can know that."

"Someone else already knows."

"It's unimportant. They'll tell no one else. The important thing is, Mose needs you to feed him. I don't think at this point he would let anyone else do it. And he needs me to protect him. We have to work together. Can we do that?"

◆

Sitting on the floor across from her husband, Kebi held her breath. She had known Amram wouldn't be completely happy with her returning to nurse Mose, but she had no idea this would be his reaction.

For a long time he said nothing, silently thinking through the situation. This part of him had always frustrated her, since she generally blurted out every thought that entered her head. For her, talking things through and thinking things through were one and the same.

But not Amram. She'd often wished she could know his thoughts—but never more than this moment.

"This is a bad idea."

Or maybe she didn't want to know his thoughts. "Why do you say that?"

"Every time you bring home news from the palace, this whole situation gets worse."

"I don't understand what you mean." As long as she could continue to nourish Mose, with her body and her words, it was fine as far as she was concerned.

"First, we decided to hide him. Then, after I heard from El Shaddai, we decided to put him in the river to be taken to an Egyptian mother who would love and care for him. At that point, you were content to trust him to Shaddai."

Content wasn't the word she'd use, but she understood what he meant.

"Then you found out the princess had him, and she asked you to nurse him, to keep him here until he was weaned." He smiled. He must have been remembering the days that Tovyah had been able to spend with them. "That was good, a gift from Shaddai. You took him to her once every ten days." His face clouded. "Then you had to leave us for fifteen days, and we limped along without you. When you returned, the princess wanted him to live with her, and you agreed to go every day. And we've managed to live with that as well."

Kebi squirmed as he recited the events of the past year and a half. The way he said it, it sounded horrible. But what else could she have done? At what point should she have made a different decision?

"Two days ago, you were ready to let him go. You were more at peace than I have seen you since before he was born. Before the green star appeared in the sky."

"I wasn't at peace! I was mourning."

"Yet now, you're ready to jump back into the same situation you have complained about often."

"I'm just not ready to let go yet. I can still teach him."

Amram fixed his dark eyes on her. "Is that really your reason? Are you doing this for him, or for you?"

Kebi played with her fingernails, refusing to meet his gaze.

"You said once that a mother shouldn't have to choose between her children. Well, sometimes they do. At least you do. You can stay here with Miriam and Aaron, or you can go to Mose."

"They don't need me as much."

Amram scoffed. "Are you kidding? Aaron cries at least once a day."

"He does?" She didn't know that.

"Shiphrah says he does. And Miriam is constantly asking if she's 'done it right.' She tries to do everything you do. But she can't, and she thinks she has failed us." He rose, looking down on her. "I won't tell you what to do. You have to make a choice. I pray you make the right one." He stomped up the stairs to the roof.

Kebi blinked back hot tears. If she went back, Miriam and Aaron could end up resenting her.

But if she stayed…

She would have plenty of time to make it up to Miriam and Aaron. But she had very little time left with Tovyah.

Why couldn't Amram see she had no choice?

◆

Kebi did her best to keep Mose from grabbing the game pieces as Ankhe and Beket set them aside.

Ankhe threw the dice. "Ha! I win!" Laughing, she moved the last piece with a hound's head through the remaining holes on her side of the board.

"Again. You've won the last six games." Beket grinned as she gathered the pieces topped with jackal heads.

"It feels so good to laugh. It's been so long." Ankhe picked up her game pieces from the low table between them and placed them into a wooden box inlaid with alternating ebony and ivory squares. "It feels like I haven't laughed in years."

This conversation was getting much too personal. Perhaps Kebi should take Mose out into the courtyard.

"Not once? You must have had some happy times," Beket said.

"Some quiet times, maybe. Some not-so-awful times." A beautiful smile came over her face. "I adore Tut. I truly do. When it's just the two of us, we actually enjoy each other."

Kebi's stomach soured. Siblings—even half-siblings—marrying one another was something she would never understand. She understood they wanted to keep the bloodlines pure, bring as much legitimacy to the throne as possible. But if they weren't always trying to conquer and subdue other people, perhaps they wouldn't need to convince everyone the king was a god.

At least Kebi thought so, but who cared what the slaves thought?

"But as soon as we arrived here, Ay began pushing us to do everything we could to discredit Father's decree to worship only the Aten. And to produce an heir." She laid her hand softly—protectively—on her stomach.

Kebi caught Beket's eye and pointed to the courtyard.

Beket nodded, and Kebi took Mose's hand.

"Little Mose! Come here." Ankhe extended her arms, leaning forward.

Mose toddled over to her, and Ankhe wrapped him in a sweet embrace. "I'll see you later, habibi."

Kebi guided him outside to the open, tiled area.

He ran to the wooden horse with a string attached to its head and began pulling it behind him.

Kebi waited in the shade of the portico, unable to get Ankhe's gesture out of her mind. Was she pregnant? That would certainly explain her sudden interest in Beket and Mose. Every time Kebi had seen her on the east bank, she'd bolted. She'd wanted nothing to do with her sister or her nephew.

But now… She'd visited at least three times a week since she first came by at the end of inundation.

She heard Ankhe say her goodbyes, and soon Beket appeared on the porch next to her.

"You'll never guess what Ankhe just told me."

"She's pregnant?" Kebi clapped her hand over her mouth. She hadn't meant to talk about the queen in such familiar terms.

Beket's eyes widened. "How could you know that?"

"Little things she's been doing. It wasn't until today I was fairly certain."

Beket laughed. "Well, you were right. It seems she conceived during the Festival of Opet, and she is now convinced she will have a son who will be Egypt's greatest king since time began."

Kebi only nodded. Was she supposed to laugh as well? Agree with the queen's prophecy?

"I shall pray she has an uneventful pregnancy and a safe birth."

"Thank you. I don't know what will happen if she loses another baby. She nearly fell apart last time. They'd sacrificed and prayed and used magic amulets—nothing worked."

Because an idol has no power.

Beket sighed. "I prayed to the Aten as well, but even he couldn't help her. Sometimes I wonder…" She shook her head.

"What?"

"I wonder about all the gods. Can any of them really do anything?" She turned and walked away before Kebi could answer her.

Maybe that was wise.

At least she was wondering. Maybe before Kebi left for good she could tell the princess about El Shaddai.

CHAPTER TWENTY

The Lord is with me; I will not be afraid.
What can mere mortals do to me?
~ Psalm 118:6 (NIV) ~

APEP, THIRD MONTH OF SHEMU, THE SEASON OF HARVEST

Warmer days had come, and the harvest was more than half completed. The scents of fresh-cut wheat and barley drifted on the air, and the Nile crept closer to its lowest level of the year.

Kebi remained under the portico while Beket and Ankhe strolled around the edges of the courtyard, talking and laughing softly. Actually, Beket strolled. Ankhe waddled. She'd almost certainly deliver before the week was over.

Ankhe had visited nearly every day for the last four months, and she had fallen completely in love with Mose. Neither Beket nor Ankhe had a mother still alive, and they had come to rely on one another.

As they turned the corner on the far side of the yard, Ankhe doubled over, grabbing Beket's arm.

Kebi ran to the pair. With Ankhe still doubled over, Kebi looked to Beket. "Is it the baby?"

"I think so. You would know better than I would."

Water splashed onto the tile, covering Ankhe's jeweled sandals.

"This baby's coming." Kebi grabbed her other arm. "We need to get her to her room."

Ankhe stood, panting, the contraction over for now. Soon her breathing returned to normal. "Not my rooms. The birthing shelter, at the edge of the palace."

"Do you know where that is?" Kebi asked Beket.

She nodded. They gently steered Ankhe back inside.

Hannah rushed over, stopping before the queen. "Can I help? Can I bring you anything?"

Beket glared. "Take care of Mose."

The trio hurried as fast as Ankhe could manage, through Beket's reception hall, across the walkway, and down the long palace halls. Halfway to the eastern doors, the sounds of whispering and frantic footsteps caused Kebi to look over her shoulder. Beket's maids—including Hannah—hurried along behind them. What had Hannah done with Mose?

The doorkeeper's face lost all color when he saw his young queen in distress. He stood as still as a pillar, apparently frozen with fright.

Ankhe cried out as another contraction washed over her, holding on to Beket and Kebi.

"Open the door!" Beket barked at the young man as soon as the contraction passed, and he hurried to obey.

Kebi almost gasped when they stepped into a lush, open area. Date palms, their gnarled trucks holding aloft massive leaves, offered abundant shade. A few anemones splashed dots of bright red here and there. Tucked in the center of a small misshapen circle of palms stood a shelter made of white linen draped over tall poles of bundled reeds.

Beket and Kebi led the queen toward the enclosure. Almost there, Kebi steadied Ankhe before moving to the opening and holding aside the fabric. Inside waited an ornate birthing chair. Wooden and decorated with gold, the seat was U-shaped, allowing the woman to rest comfortably instead of squatting, yet still permit the babe to slip unhindered from her body and give the midwife room to work.

Beket led the queen inside.

Ankhe groaned loudly for a moment, eyes shut tight, face twisted with pain, her arms cradling her belly. Once the contraction had eased, she leaned forward, her weight on her arms on the chair, then twisted to lower herself to a seated position. She tried to remove her bracelets, but her hands were trembling.

Kebi reached to help her remove them. "Would you like your necklace off as well?" she whispered.

Ankhe nodded and Kebi moved behind the younger woman to reach the clasp of the heavy, jeweled necklace she wore. Beket bent to untie her belt, and Kebi removed her sandals.

Maia burst into the tent, another woman about her age with her. "I've brought the midwife." She looked at Kebi, her face for once free of condemnation. "You." She pointed at Kebi and stepped nearer. "You've given birth. If it's all right with Ankhe, you may stay." She turned toward the attendants, including Hannah. "The rest of you, out." Maia shooed them toward the opening.

Hannah aimed a glare at Kebi, as if she were somehow responsible for Hannah's dismissal.

Maia wandered around the tent, an ivory wand made from the tusk of a hippo in hand, muttering incantations to the gods that had been placed strategically in the tent beforehand.

The birth proceeded slowly. Kebi knelt near Ankhe's head, reassuring her every time something new happened that it was quite normal.

Kebi knew the pain of losing a baby. Whether or not Ankhe worshipped El Shaddai, whether or not her husband had commanded Hebrew babies be slaughtered while Egyptian babies lived, Kebi didn't want the queen to experience another devastating loss.

Shaddai, please let this new prince—or princess—live.

◆

The sun had nearly finished its path through the sky, dipping behind the palace and rendering the garden a tiny bit cooler. The delivery dragged on, and Kebi needed to nurse Mose. She excused herself, rushed to Beket's rooms, tended to Mose, and hurried back. Neferet had been watching over him, and for once Kebi was happy he didn't need her.

She was almost to the tent when she heard the palace door open behind her. She turned to see a disheveled Tut step tentatively into the courtyard. He looked nothing like a king. At this moment, he was only an anxious husband. She could tell him that all day was nothing when it came time to birthing a baby, but after last time...

She moved to the side and waited, head bowed, beneath a palm, allowing him to pass her.

Tut crept toward the tent, worry and pain contorting his face. He was but a few strides from the shelter when Hannah stepped away from her self-appointed position at the curtained door, halting before the king.

"The queen is not to be interrupted. You must go."

"But, please—"

"No." Hannah placed her hands on her hips, holding her ground.

Kebi held her breath.

Hannah seemed very proud of herself for having treated Egypt's god on earth like a child. She'd become extraordinarily protective of Ankhe for whatever reason, but this was unbelievable. Tut could order her death where she stood. Fortunately for her, only one thing was on his mind.

But later, would he remember?

Hannah returned to her position.

Tut remained alone, mouth gaping. Shoulders slumped, he trudged toward the palace doors but caught Kebi's gaze as he passed her. He paused a moment, then neared her. "Can you tell me, please, is my wife well?"

She dipped her head. "My king, the last time I was in the tent, she was doing well. The birth is taking longer than you might expect, but I assure you this is perfectly normal."

His face relaxed a bit. "Thank you." He headed for the door. Just as he reached for it, an agonizing screech came from the tent. Tut spun around, panic written all over his face.

Kebi turned to see the midwife peer from the shelter to beckon her.

The queen slumped on the chair, silent sobs rocking her body, hands covering her face, an unmoving form at her feet.

Not again.

Such loss at so young an age. Home, god, name. Mother, father, sisters—and two children.

Maia gently wrapped a cloth around the baby girl and picked it up, cradling it as if it were still alive, and brought it to Kebi. Tears collected on the older woman's lashes. Was she remembering her own daughter? "Go to the main palace. Head straight down the hall. Someone will stop you soon enough. Tell them you need to see the royal embalmer."

"Yes, Maia." Kebi left the tent quickly, as quietly as possible.

Tut, pacing under the palms, crumpled at the sight of the bundle in Kebi's arms, his shoulders shaking with heart-rending cries.

She slipped quickly around him. By the time she reached the door he was demanding to see Ankhe.

Memories of holding an unmoving baby Benjamin haunted Kebi's thoughts. But now was the time to concentrate on Ankhe. Was there anything Kebi could say, could do, to ease her pain?

No.

She hurried down the long columned hall. The palace's bright colors seemed subdued today.

After only a few steps, she saw Mahu's unmistakable silhouette, his headdress and broad shoulders, farther down the hall.

Thank You, Shaddai.

She hastened toward him. He was in the middle of a conversation, and she didn't want anyone else to gawk at the princess. She hid behind a pillar, where she could still hear their voices though she couldn't see them. When they quieted, she stepped out.

Mahu nearly bumped into her. He stared at the babe in her arms, then raised pain-filled eyes to her. "No," he whispered.

She nodded. "Maia will need you tonight."

"Come." He led her down the main hallway and turned right, down a narrow aisle to its end. He opened a door to the outside, the building where the barber worked across a narrow path. They followed hallway after hallway until they reached the farthest corner. He held the door open for her.

She passed him and stepped into a room far more expansive than it appeared from the outside. Men in colored linen robes moved busily about. Soft chanting filled the room. Strange potions in ivory jars lined the shelves.

Mahu stood behind her.

Soon a wide, pudgy man approached them. "Captain?" His voice was surprisingly soft, probably from years of dealing with grieving loved ones.

Mahu gestured to the precious bundle in Kebi's arms. "The princess has passed over to the other realm."

The man's face remained expressionless. "We'll take excellent care of her."

Kebi extended her arms, and the embalmer gently took the infant from her.

Unexpected emptiness slammed into her. Why did she feel so hollow? This wasn't her baby. She felt empty enough whenever she thought about leaving Mose. She didn't need the grief of another adding to her own.

But she was a mother, and it seemed a mother's heart was made to harbor pain—anyone's pain. Whether she wanted to or not.

◆

Paenipat, Second Month of Akhet, The Season of Inundation

The last seventy days in the palace had been somber, tense, and gloomy. It was as if an enormous black cloud had descended on the palace.

No one had seen Ankhe since she'd left the birthing tent.

Tut himself was rarely seen. He had dismissed the loud, official mourners within the first hour. Servants made as little noise as possible while carrying out their duties. The palace officials holed up in their rooms. All official visits by foreign dignitaries had been canceled, though gifts poured in from faraway rulers, lower administrators throughout Egypt, and peasants alike.

They sat untouched in a corner of the audience hall.

Kebi arrived as early as possible on the seventieth day. Having never attended or even seen an Egyptian funeral, she had no idea what lay ahead.

Beket and Mose waited in the main room when Kebi arrived. Her attendants hugged the walls. No one wore makeup or jewelry, only a bleached white tunic.

Beket approached her. "I'd like you to walk with me in the procession. If my brother needs me, I want you to stay with Mose."

"Yes, nebet-i."

"And will you carry these?" She handed Kebi a necklace much like the one Kebi had worn when she began nursing Mose. Kebi's chest tightened when she saw a miniature cartouche, engraved with what must be the tiny princess's name, dangling from a short length of gold chain.

Maia came from her room, dressed as the others. She nodded at Beket and headed for the main door to the walkway. Kebi followed Beket, who tucked Mose's little hand in hers. The handmaidens brought up the rear.

They crossed the walkway to the palace and entered the audience hall. Hundreds of people milled around the room. As if waiting for Beket, a priest moved to the front of the room and stood next to the throne. Every visible part of his body was shaved. A leopard skin robe, head draped over one shoulder, designated him as the highest priest of Amun, with power second only to Tut and Ay.

An assistant, wearing only a tunic but hairless as well, banged a drum, and the chief priest called for silence.

The sea of mourners parted, creating a wide aisle down the center of the long hall. Kebi backed up and found her place next to Mose, Beket on his other side.

A Mother's Sacrifice: Jochebed's Story

All eyes turned to the back of the room. The miniature coffin was small enough to be carried by one priest. A pair of women representing the goddess Isis and her sister Nephthys walked behind him, followed by yet another priest with a chest. The jeweled box would contain the internal organs of the princess, each one—except for the heart—removed from the body and placed in a special pottery jar.

Tut and Ankhe entered the hall. Tut hadn't shaved during the mourning period. He crooked a finger at Beket, who hurried to his side. His arm around her waist, he pulled her close.

The sight of Ankhe sent a familiar stab of pain through Kebi's heart. Nothing in the world compared to the indescribable pain of losing a child.

Ankhe was pale. Her eyes were sunken, with dark circles under them. She'd lost a good deal of weight, her unadorned tunic draping loosely on her. One hand clasping her husband's, the other reaching across her body to clutch his arm, she clung to Tut as if he held her next breath.

The head priest led the group out of the hall, out of the palace, and into the desert. Another priest waved burning incense and yet another sprinkled milk along the path.

Kebi looked back at the swarm of people behind them. Friends, servants, and officials carried gifts meant to help the dead in the afterlife. Paid mourners and more priests completed the parade.

Kebi reached for Mose's hand. He could easily get lost in this crowd. A short walk under the blistering sun brought them to the tomb Tut had been preparing for himself. His first daughter, stillborn at only five months, had been placed inside little more than a year earlier. The group gathered as the priests took their places at the tomb's opening, and Kebi found a place near Beket, still comforting Tut and Ankhe.

Mose tugged on her tunic. "Up." He raised his arms, and Kebi picked him up so he could see what was happening. "I want Aunt Ankhe." He reached toward her.

"We can't right now. But later you can give her a big hug. She is very sad." Kebi kept her voice low.

"Why is she sad?"

What to say? "The baby that was in her tummy is gone."

"Baby is gone?" His mouth screwed up, and he wrapped his arms around her neck, softly crying. Ankhe had often talked to him about how her baby and Mose would play together.

A priest read prayers to honor the princess and performed spells to see her safely to the other side. Dancers and musicians performed. Mourners cried loudly, pulling their hair out.

It was difficult to hear, and the Egyptian was full of words unfamiliar to Kebi.

Maia came to stand next to her. "The prince needs to understand what is happening. May I explain it to him? I know you can't."

Though it sounded like one of her daily criticisms, Maia's voice held none of the harshness Kebi had come to expect.

"Of course." Kebi transferred Mose to her arms.

Maia pointed to the priest, who removed the mummy from the box and held it upright. "See what he is doing? It's very important. The mouth clamps shut after death, and it must be pried open so the person can eat, and drink, and breathe in the afterlife."

Kebi squeezed her hands together to avoid rebutting what Maia taught him. This was not the time.

More anointing and prayers and spells. The objects brought by others were presented so the princess could use them. Patiently and simply, Maia explained everything to Mose as it happened.

"Beket gave me this. Would you go with him to take it up?" Kebi held up the necklace Beket had given her.

"Why don't you and Mose do it?"

Maia would trust her with this? "Me? Don't you want to take him?"

Maia smiled softly—the first genuine smile she had ever given Kebi. "I've given more gifts at funerals than I care to count. You help Mose bless his cousin." She set him on the ground and bent low. "Mose, will you take this and place it with the other gifts for the baby?" She held up a carved ivory doll.

"A doll?"

"This is a *shabti*. Everyone is required to work in the afterlife. This doll will do the princess's work for her."

Mose took the doll, and Kebi led him to the growing pile of shabti dolls, clothing, shoes, jewelry, furniture, food, drink—anything she could possibly need to make her life in the other realm more enjoyable. It would all be placed in the tomb alongside the coffin.

Mose looked up at Kebi, hesitating.

"Go on," she said.

He stepped forward and laid the necklace and the doll on a tiny, ornate bed.

Kebi took Mose's hand. She turned to see King Tut nod at her. Beket mouthed, "Thank you."

At the sight of Ankhe, Mose ran to her instead. Kebi hurried after him. "Mose! No!" she whispered as loudly as possible.

But Ankhe knelt and pulled him close. "Thank you, habibi."

Kebi waited until the queen released him, kissing his cheek, then whisked him away.

As she walked Mose back to their places, she tried to ignore the fact that she had just helped Mose take a huge step closer to becoming a true Egyptian.

◆

Kebi pulled a linen blanket up over Mose as he slept. The day had been long and hot, and except for a short period in the afternoon when his exhaustion took over, he'd done beautifully. She kissed his forehead. She couldn't wait to get home and hug her children.

She gathered her things and entered Beket's receiving hall but halted in the doorway. Tut stared at his sister, arms crossed, six Medjay behind him.

The last time he brought guards with him to Beket's rooms, he brought the astrologer to see if Mose should be killed. What could he want this time?

Their voices were too low. She crept along the wall, closer to the pair.

"You can't be serious!" Beket's hands were fisted at her side, red creeping up her neck.

"I am."

"You can't do this!" Her voice rose, her body trembled.

He stepped nearer. "I can and I will. I will do whatever is necessary."

"Brother, habibi, please!" She reached for him, but Medjay instantly surrounded him. One stepped between them, hand on his short ax. Another, still at the door, reached for an arrow.

"I will return tomorrow morning." The king turned and left, his guards backing out, eyes on Beket.

Beket fell to the ground, her hands covering her face.

Kebi dropped her bag and rushed to her. "Beket! What happened?" She wrapped her arms around the princess, who was still shaking uncontrollably.

Neferet approached them, eyes wide. "What's wrong?"

Kebi shrugged. "Get Maia."

Neferet bolted, returning soon with the nurse.

Maia knelt on Beket's other side. Neither of them could calm her.

Long moments later, her tears spent, Beket sat up. Her eyes were bloodshot, her face blotchy.

"What happened?" Maia asked.

Beket stared into space.

"Beket?" Maia took her hand.

The princess drew in a shuddering breath. "He said the physicians have said Ankhe will never have children."

Terrible news but not enough to cause this kind of anguish.

"And…?" Kebi asked.

"He wants Mose."

CHAPTER TWENTY-ONE

*Hear my prayer, L*ORD*; let my cry for help come to you.*
Do not hide your face from me when I am in distress.
Turn your ear to me; when I call, answer me quickly.
~ Psalm 102:1–2 (NIV) ~

Kebi and Amram sat against the wall, silent. Miriam and Aaron had been put to bed, even though the sun wasn't remotely close to setting. The days lasted so long this time of year they wouldn't get enough rest if they slept only when it was dark.

Besides, Kebi and Amram needed some time alone.

"He just came right out and said that?" asked Amram. "That he was going to take Tovyah away from his sister and claim him as his son?"

Kebi shrugged. "He is 'the living image of Amun.' He is, for everyday purposes, a god. He can do whatever he wants."

"Of course, but this... To his own sister, his only blood sister? You would think..." He blew out a long breath.

The image of Ankhe earlier at the funeral—drawn, silent, ashen—hovered in the back of her mind. "I think he and Ankhesenamun are beside themselves with grief. They were so certain this baby would survive, had been specially blessed by

Amun. When it was taken away from them, without a sound, without a whimper…and then to be told there will never be another baby. I think it's more than she can bear. And as strange as it is to us, I believe he truly loves her. I think he would do anything if he thought it would take away her pain."

"I know how he feels. But these are things that are best left to El Shaddai. Only He can give life—or take it."

Kebi leaned her head on his shoulder. "I know."

Amram twisted to face her. "You seem to be taking this very well. Why are you so calm?" He narrowed his eyes at her.

"Don't worry. I have no devious plans."

"I wasn't suggesting that."

How did she explain it? She didn't truly understand it herself. "I think I've lost him so many times already. When Shiphrah told me about the edict. When Mahu saw him. When I put him in the water. When he called Beket 'Muu.' When she sent me home… But El Shaddai had a plan. Every time, He had a better plan than I could ever have imagined."

"True."

"Tut said he'd come back for him tomorrow." Tears blurred her vision.

Amram kissed her temple. "I think all we can do is trust that He will carry out His plan." He reached for her hand. "Pray with me?"

She nodded.

Amram leaned forward on his arms, tucked his legs under his body, and placed his head on the ground.

Kebi carefully imitated him.

"God of our fathers Abraham, Isaac, and Jacob," said Amram, "we come to You, on our faces, to plead for our son, Your servant Tovyah, who has also been named Mose.

"We trust You will do as You have promised, and that when it is time, He will remember all we have taught him about You. That he will know everything he needs to know to save Israel from this hateful bondage. Until then, we ask that You protect him from the false gods of Egypt."

Amram sniffled. "Like Jacob, when he was in Beersheba, we cry 'Here I am.' We are here to do whatever You ask. If that means allowing"—his voice choked—"him to go with the king, then we will trust You to watch over him."

Kebi had never prayed aloud in front of Amram, though he'd prayed over her many times. She gathered up what little courage she had. "God of our fathers, I cannot bear the thought of my little Tovyah being raised by the man who ordered his death." Hot tears flooded her face, and she reached for Amram's hand. "So I, too, pray as Jacob did and say, 'I will not let You go unless You bless me.' I beg You to give me Your peace. Teach me to trust You, in this more than anything else."

She fell silent. There were not enough words to express everything she had held inside for so long. Love. Jealousy. Joy. Bitterness. Fear. Emptiness.

Slowly, the emotions that had become so entangled with each other for over two years began to separate, and the fear began to lift.

Trust replaced it, filling up all the desolate empty spaces in her heart.

It was deep into the night when Kebi finally fell asleep, like Jacob, in the presence of Shaddai.

◆

It wasn't until this very moment that Kebi realized how passionately Beket loved Mose.

The princess paced, chewing on her nails. She wore yesterday's tunic, her face still devoid of makeup, her hair hanging loose. Had she slept at all? She looked nearly as bad as Ankhe had yesterday.

Only Neferet accompanied Beket today. The slender maid hovered helplessly in the background, wringing her hands.

Beket's slow footsteps and the water of the clock trickling from one jar to another were the only sounds. At every noise, no matter how slight, Beket looked toward the door, panic written across her face.

"Where is he?" Beket angrily wiped the tears from her cheeks. "He's trying to make this as painful as possible."

Kebi stood nearby, her arms wrapped around her middle, trying to ignore her own pain and concentrate on Beket's. She would lose Mose eventually, but Beket still had a chance.

Was there anything Kebi could say to ease it? Losing a child was losing a child, whether that child was still and silent at birth, slipped away a few months later—or was put under a sentence of death.

Suddenly Beket halted and faced Kebi. Bringing a hand to her mouth, the princess hurried to Kebi. "Oh, Jochebed. I am so sorry. I know now how you must have felt when you put Mose in the water." She grasped Kebi's hands and drew them to her chest. "Please forgive me for all the horribly thoughtless things I must have said to you."

Kebi searched the princess's face. Such anguish, especially for one who had rarely been told no, seldom not achieved what she pursued. "I'm sorry too. I said some awful things about you."

"I don't remember that."

Kebi smiled weakly. "I said them at home."

Beket squeezed her hands. "I can't say that I blame you."

A knock sounded. All eyes turned to the door.

Tension filled the main hall like the Nile's waters filled the canals. Beket stared at the door, her feet frozen to the floor by fear—no, not fear. Sheer unadulterated dread.

Tut had always just walked in. It was his sister's suite of rooms, and he was the king, after all. Until now, they'd been extremely close. Beket was devoted to him, would do anything to help him.

Except this.

◆

Kebi moved her hand to Beket's back while Neferet opened the door.

Tut stood alone in the doorway. No Medjay. No servants. He stepped inside and strode to face Beket.

Beket's lip quivered, her body trembled.

Tut lifted his chin, stared at her unblinking. "I have come for the child."

The king had grown since the first time Kebi saw him, nearly two years ago. He was bulkier, more muscled. Taller—as tall as Beket now. He was no longer the boy king. He was the ruler of the most powerful nation on earth.

How did you say no to a king?

"Produce the child." Tut's voice was monotone. Not like that of someone eager to pour love into someone's life.

"Please, no. Please reconsider, I beg you." She stepped closer to her brother, clasping her hands at her chest.

"Produce the child."

"The child? The *child*? Can't you even say his name? Is he to be your son, or just an heir? Whose idea is this, yours or Ankhe's?" Beket's eyes grew wide, and she took one more step toward him. "Or Vizier Ay's?"

"It is none of your concern."

"Not my concern? He's my son!"

Would the king punish his own sister for her insolence? Or would he show her mercy as he took her son from her?

Kebi leaned closer to whisper in her ear. "Beket… Do you want to argue with the king?"

"Yes, I do. I would rather die than give my son to him!"

Tut huffed. "He's not even your son."

"I am the only mother he will ever remember!" Tears finally flooded Beket's face.

Kebi ignored the pain that sliced through her heart.

"You obviously don't care about him, but how can you do this to me?"

"I will do what I must to ensure this kingdom never falls." He dropped his eyes. "No matter who it hurts."

El Shaddai, please protect my son, her son.

CHAPTER TWENTY-TWO

✦

He will cover you with his feathers, and under his wings you will find refuge; his faithfulness will be your shield and rampart.

~ Psalm 91:4 (NIV) ~

Maia barged through the doors in the back of the hall and strode toward Tut. She jabbed one finger at his chest, stopping just short of touching him. "Is this how I taught you?"

Some of the arrogance faded from Tut's face.

"Wherever did you get such a horrific idea? Children are not pets, like your dog. You can't rip him from this life, from the only mother he knows."

Kebi groaned silently. But Maia was right. Beket was Mose's mother now, the only one he would know as Mother, call Mother.

Tut lifted his chin. "I can do whatever I wish. I am the Son of Ra, the Living Image of Amun."

"Yes, you are. And I would expect better behavior from the image of our god." Maia stared up at the man she'd raised. "Do you truly want to destroy your sister to give your wife something that, in the long run, will not make her happy?"

Tut threw a hand in the air. "Why won't it? This child is not Beket's either. Why can't he bring to Ankhe the same joy he brought to Beket?"

Beket reached for Kebi's hand.

"Because Beket did not *steal* the child. She did not take a baby from his mother *against her will*. Is that what you want to do? Do you want to someday explain that to Mose?"

There will be enough to explain as it is.

"I will do what I have to." He closed his eyes. Sighed. "I can't watch her cry anymore." His voice was softer, sadder.

"So this is not for the kingdom. This is for her."

He nodded.

"This child will not heal you, or Ankhe. The guilt in your heart will not allow it. He can never be your heir. He is not your blood. He is Hebrew."

"Then what do I do for her?" He looked more like the distraught husband Kebi had seen in the courtyard.

"Did *she* ask for this?" Maia placed a hand on his chest.

He shook his head. "No. She didn't. She wouldn't."

"Then go to her. Love her. Comfort her. The pain will never go away, but it will lessen, I promise you."

Maia spoke from experience. Kebi could hear the pain in her voice. The pain of losing Benjamin had diminished for Kebi, but was still there. Would the pain of losing Mose also subside, eventually?

Tut nodded and turned to go.

"Before you go, tell me," said Maia. "How did you come up with this plan?"

He thought a moment. Paced several strides away before turning back again. "Ankhe hasn't come from her rooms in her palace since the funeral. I went to see her one day. I wasn't sure if she was asleep, or awake... I waited outside her bedroom. Her attendant was bathing her and talking to Ankhe, though Ankhe didn't respond. The maid was telling her she'd heard that Beket had said she regretted keeping the boy."

Beket gasped. "I *never* said that." Her voice rumbled as she strained to keep it free from anger.

Tut frowned at her, his brow furrowed. "She said you never spent any time with him, that you ignored him and let his nurse have complete charge of his day. That you could barely spare time to kiss him good night."

Who would say such evil things? Kebi could painfully attest that Beket spent every moment she could with Mose.

Beket locked her gaze on Kebi. "That is entirely untrue." She turned back to Tut. "So at this point you decided you could take better care of him than I can?"

"I just wanted Ankhe to stop crying. To be happy."

"Who is the girl who fabricated such lies?" asked Beket.

He scoffed. "I barely know the names of my own attendants, let alone the queen's."

Maia stepped forward. "We need to find out. Can you summon her?"

"I can try." He turned to go.

"Quickly, please." Maia called after him.

Beket touched Kebi on the arm. "I am so sorry about that," she whispered. "You more than anyone know how much I love him, that I don't regret keeping him."

"I know. I don't regret it either."

For possibly the first time, she truly meant it.

◆

Neferet answered the door to a Medjay accompanying a young girl. "The king has sent this servant to you. He has remained with the queen."

"You are the one who said the princess regretted taking Mose as her son?" asked Maia.

The servant bowed her head. "I am." Her eyes were as round as plums, her shoulders shaking.

"And why would you say such things?" demanded Maia.

"It's what I was told! I would never say anything I did not believe to be true."

"And who told you they were true?" Maia's voice gentled considerably.

"One of your attendants. I assumed she would know the truth."

"Who?" Beket grabbed the girl's arm. "Who told you I do not love my son?"

Maia placed a hand on Beket's, and she let go.

Kebi wrapped an arm around Beket and gently led her away from the terrified servant.

"Who told you these lies?" Maia asked.

"Her name is Hannah." The girl's voice was so low she could barely be understood.

Beket beckoned to Maia. "Bring me Hannah. And Mose."

Maia left the main hall.

"And when did she tell you these things?" asked Beket.

"I first met her on the barque, on the way to the festival. Over the months she has told me many things."

"Such as?" asked Beket.

"She said you had, on more than one occasion, mentioned you should have left him in the river, as your maids suggested."

Kebi stared at the mosaic on the floor. Knowing it wasn't true made it no easier hearing it.

Maia joined them, Mose on her hip, Hannah behind her.

Beket crossed the growing circle of people and stood before Hannah. "Did you tell this one"—she pointed at Ankhe's servant—"that I spend no time with my son? That I do not love him?"

"I did."

Beket took Mose and whispered once again to Maia, who headed for the main door, then Beket turned to Ankhe's servant. "You may return to the queen. What she does with you is her concern, but other than believing a liar, I find no fault with you."

The Medjay gripped her arm and led her away.

Beket huffed. "Why? Why would you do this?"

Hannah turned her cold stare to Kebi. "To hurt you."

Kebi stepped backward, her hand to her heart. "Me? Why? What have I done to you to cause such hate?"

"My mother is Elisheba."

"There are many named Elisheba." Even as she said it, Kebi knew which Elisheba she was talking about.

"*Joel's* Elisheba." Hannah continued to drill a stare into Kebi.

Kebi's blood ran cold. *Elli.* This was all because of Elli.

"But I don't remember a daughter named Hannah."

"My name is Shoshanna."

Little Shoshanna? She looked completely different than the young girl who had once lived on their street.

Beket stepped between them. "I don't understand. Who is Elisheba?"

The muscles in Hannah's neck tightened. "My mother had her only son ripped from her arms by the Medjay. My baby brother screamed as they pulled on him. She begged. The Medjay didn't care, and he didn't stop!" She paused and calmed herself. "I wasn't there. I married and moved to another village years ago. But she told me about it, when she could get through the story without falling apart. She hasn't been the same since."

That much was true. "But I was not responsible for that. Why do you feel you need to hurt me?" Kebi searched the girl's face for any sign of remorse or compassion.

She found none.

"My mother told me what you did."

"That I put Mose in the basket?"

"That you brought him back to the village, told everyone how wonderful El Shaddai was to give you back your son."

"Should I not have praised El Shaddai for what He did?"

"You should have suffered like she did!" She stomped closer, fists by her shoulders, much like a toddler in the midst of a tantrum.

Maia shoved the front door open. Mahu marched behind her.

"Did your mother send you?" asked Kebi.

Hannah glanced at Mahu, now standing behind Kebi, arms crossed. She drew in a breath through her nose. "She knows I'm here. She knows you're here. But she knew nothing of my plan. Really, I had no plan when I came here. I just wanted to see the woman who ruined my mother's life."

"How did *I* ruin her life?" asked Kebi.

"You are the one who reminded her of her loss, every day, every night."

Realization slowly crept into Kebi's mind. "It was you who told Beket I was Mose's mother."

Hannah smirked. "I was. And you were banished from his presence." The smile faded. "For three days. Then you decided you could both love him, care for him, and it was worse than before. And after the festival, I mentioned to the princess how hard it must be to see him only once a week. That it was too bad she couldn't have him here all week."

Kebi's chest ached. Hannah was responsible for Tovyah moving to the palace so soon. Responsible for Kebi being sent home. Now this was her doing as well.

Kebi scoffed. "Shouldn't you be angry at the king? Or even the princess?"

"After the funeral, with Ankhe's baby gone, the princess came back with Mose, just like you had done in the village. I decided then I could make everyone pay for what had happened to my imma. I couldn't do much to the king, but he would at least lose his sister. The princess would lose Mose.

Mose would likely never accept the queen as his mother, so she would lose him as well. And no matter what, you would never see him again."

Kebi shook her head. "So you came here, lived here for a year, just to take vengeance for your mother?"

"My husband died shortly after we were married. We had no children. I stayed with his parents because he was their only son and they had no one else. But when my mother told me what happened... I love my mother, more than anything. I had to do something. Besides, even slaves eat better and live better here than in the villages."

Anger replaced Kebi's pity. "You have no idea what it is like to be a mother. A mother could never do this."

Mahu stepped forward. "You will be put in a cell until the princess decides what to do with you."

Hannah backed away. "I didn't *do* anything worthy of prison. All I did was lie a little."

Mahu frowned. "The princess disagrees."

Beket stood and approached Hannah. "You used my son to satisfy your own desire for vengeance." Her voice was barely controlled. "You put a prince in danger."

Hannah held out a hand in a useless attempt to ward off the Medjay. "I didn't put him in danger. You can't hold me responsible for what others did."

"We can. And we do." Mahu reached the girl in one long stride. He wrapped a hand around her upper arm and dragged her away.

"No! Wait!" Hannah's cries faded as Mahu led her from Beket's palace.

◆

Kebi moved Mose's hands from the table so the attendant could set the food down for their afternoon meal. The shade of the portico was pleasant, and the chaos of the morning had faded. A quiet afternoon awaited.

Neferet appeared, her face pale. "Nebet-i, the king wishes to see you." For a brief moment, fear flashed on Beket's face.

"You may send him in."

Neferet stepped aside, and Tut appeared in the doorway. "May I come in?"

Kebi pulled Mose onto her lap as she watched Beket's face. Surely he wouldn't ask permission if he'd changed his mind, if he'd come back for Mose.

The king ambled slowly toward them. "I am sorry for the pain I caused. I—I just wanted Ankhe to stop crying. I love her so much.... It killed me to see her so distraught. I didn't think about anyone else."

Beket rose to embrace him. "Thank you, brother."

Mose jumped down from Kebi's lap and grabbed Tut's hand. "I see Aunt Ankhe?"

A sad smile crossed Tut's face. He squeezed Mose's hand. "Not today, habibi. But she misses you, very much. Perhaps in a few days."

Mose backed up and leaned against Kebi's legs.

"I need to get back to her. Maybe you can come visit later?" Tut asked.

"Of course."

He turned and left the room.

Beket smiled, more relaxed than she'd been in weeks. "I guess everything is back to the way it was. Just in time for Opet."

"Nebet-i, I've been thinking about Opet."

"We are back to 'my lady'?"

"I have something to tell you." A year ago, Beket had said those same words before she told her she wanted Mose to live at the palace.

"Yes?"

"I would rather not go, if I have your permission."

Beket set her goblet down. "Not go? Why not? If you don't, won't you have the same concern you had last year?"

"I won't be able to nurse him, that's true." She rose and stepped away a moment. "The reason I agreed to nurse Mose, and was ecstatic to hear your request, was because I couldn't let him go. I thought the only way to protect him was to be with him. After all, if a child isn't safe with his mother, then where can he be safe? But I've been with him, and so have you, and he was still in danger."

Beket nodded. "That's true. It's hard when you realize you can't protect them from everything, as much as you want to."

"Last night, I learned that I don't have to be with him to be a good mother. I can still care about him, pray for him… I can love him no matter where I am."

Eyes wet, Beket took Kebi's hands in hers. "You know you're welcome to stay as long as you want."

"Unless you command me to stay, I think it's time to leave him with you. He belongs here, and I belong at home." She watched Mose climbing under the table to sit near Miu.

Beket nodded, sniffling. "I'm sorry it won't be you, but he will be with a mother, a mother who loves him more than breath. And I will give my life before I let harm come to him, I promise you."

"I know. But it's not you I have to trust. I will pray for him, and *El Shaddai* will protect him."

"I envy your trust in your God. He must be very powerful."

Kebi smiled. "He is." Dare she say more? "He is the one true God. He is the living God, and not an idol of wood or gold. It is He who created all things, and He who can bring to pass what He has promised."

Beket grinned. "Perhaps I need to learn more about this God."

"Anytime you want to talk, you know where to find me."

◆

Kebi laid Mose on the bed. She had fed him for the last time. She'd nursed her other children until they were three. Mose was just over two, but he'd eaten so much better than most children she needn't worry about his health if she had to go. Goat's milk was always available, and Beket could hire another wet nurse.

"Mose, when you wake up I will be gone."

"I see you 'morrow?"

She shook her head. "No, motek. It's time for me to go to my home, to my children."

He screwed up his little mouth. "You don't come back?"

"I don't think so."

Tears filled his eyes. "I miss you, Kebi." He scrambled to his feet and hugged her, fiercely.

"I will miss you too." Her voice broke. "You have no idea how much I will miss you. But you have your muut, and she will take such good care of you."

He nodded into her neck.

She pulled him away to see his face. "Whatever happens, remember I love you. And El Shaddai loves you too."

"I 'member." He hugged her once more.

It took every bit of courage she could summon to drag herself from his room.

◆

Outside the village wall, Kebi stepped off the chariot of gold for the last time.

"I will miss carrying you to the palace each day."

"I'll miss you too, Mahu." Her throat burned. Leaving was the right thing to do, but that didn't make it easy.

"May I give you a hug?" he asked.

"Of course." She wrapped her arms around his neck. Memories of the last time she had hugged her abba surfaced. "Take care of Mose for me?"

"As though he was my own."

He meant that, she knew.

She waited until he drove away before she began the walk into the village. Clutched in her hand was a cartouche on a gold chain—engraved with the name Mose.

For the first time since Tovyah's birth, she was at peace. She still ached to hold him, but he would be well cared for. By Beket. By Mahu and Maia. Even Ankhe would shower him with love.

But most of all, El Shaddai would be with him. Every step of every day, just as He promised Jacob: "I am with you and will watch over you wherever you go, and I will bring you back to this land. I will not leave you until I have done what I have promised you."

They had named him well. *Tovyah.* God is good.

Finally, with every beat of her heart, she believed it.

CLOSING THOUGHTS FROM THE AUTHOR

✦

By faith Moses' parents hid him for three months after he was born, because they saw he was no ordinary child, and they were not afraid of the king's edict. By faith Moses, when he had grown up, refused to be known as the son of Pharaoh's daughter. He chose to be mistreated along with the people of God rather than to enjoy the fleeting pleasures of sin. He regarded disgrace for the sake of Christ as of greater value than the treasures of Egypt, because he was looking ahead to his reward. By faith he left Egypt, not fearing the king's anger; he persevered because he saw him who is invisible.
~ Hebrews 11:23–27 (NIV) ~

Scripture tells us nothing more about Jochebed or Amram. Moses spent forty years in the palace and forty more in Midian before he returned to Egypt, so it is unlikely they were alive to see him lead Israel out of Egypt. All we are certain of is that they hid Moses until they put him in the river and allowed the daughter of the pharaoh to raise him as her own.

We do know that the princess left Egypt and its false gods at some point. She sought refuge with the Israelites and came to worship El Shaddai. First Chronicles 4:18 tells us, "These were the children of Pharaoh's daughter Bithiah, whom Mered had married." Bithiah in Hebrew is Batyah—daughter of God.

Tut ruled only another six years before he mysteriously died at age nineteen. Although Tut had named his general of the armies, Horemheb, as his heir, Vizier Ay usurped the throne. Scholars believe he tried to force Ankhesenamun to marry him to strengthen his claim. It appears Ankhe wrote to the king of the Hittites, and after telling him she feared for her life, asked him to send one of his sons to marry her and become pharaoh. A prince, Zannanza, was murdered on his way to Egypt. War ensued.

Scripture praises both Jochebed and the royal daughter. Each had a different but critical role in the life of a special baby boy. Heartaches and joy alike would combine to teach both the power of a mother's love.

* * *

FACTS BEHIND *the Fiction*

PAPYRUS: THE MULTIPURPOSE REED

MOSES FLOATS ON A PLANT THAT GAVE US THE BIBLE

When Jochebed realized she couldn't hide Baby Moses any longer, she did what Pharaoh told all Hebrew midwives to do with their people's newborn boys. She put him in the Nile River.

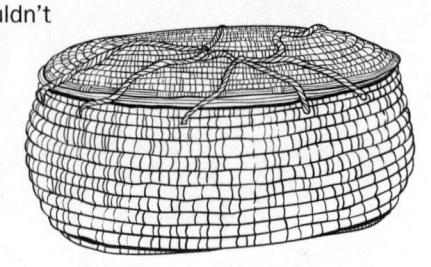

PAPYRUS REED BASKET FROM EGYPT

But she made sure he floated. "She got a basket made of papyrus reeds and waterproofed it with tar" (Exodus 2:3 NLT).

Papyrus floats. When the spongy pith inside a papyrus reed dries up, what's left is a hollowed reed filled with air. That makes it light, buoyant, and just the right material for weaving together a floating basket or even a small river boat.

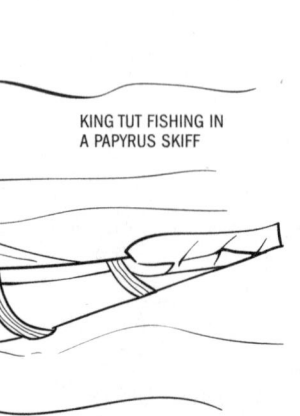

KING TUT FISHING IN A PAPYRUS SKIFF

GETTING THE MOST FROM PAPYRUS REEDS

Egyptians found plenty of ways to use papyrus stalks, which grew about ten feet high (three meters) in the quiet waters of swamps and marshes near the Nile River.

But papyrus is most famous for paper, both the word and the product.

The word *paper* comes from the Egyptian word *papyrus*. The product of papyrus paper, which replaced leather scrolls, came from the spongy, tube-shaped pith inside the reeds. Egyptians chopped down the reeds, carefully cut out the pith tube inside each one, and then sliced the tubes into long, thin strips. They crisscrossed the strips in woven, plaid-like layers to form the shape of a single page. Then they squashed the layers together under heavy stones and dried them in the sun. This paper was strong stuff, hard to tear, and easier to work with than leather scrolls. Prettier too.

Even the word *Bible* comes from this reed. Egyptians shipped papyrus paper abroad, out of one of the region's main ports: Byblos in what is now Lebanon. Greeks borrowed *Byblos* as a nickname for books: *biblos*. From that Greek word for books came *Bible*, which means "books."

Using the whole plant, from the spongy pith inside to the flexible, fibrous stalks outside, Egyptians were able to make sails for their boats, sandals for their feet, mats, lamp wicks, paintbrushes, chairs, ropes, reed pens, flutes, fish traps, roofs, and arrows. They could even chew it like gum; the root tastes sweet, a bit like licorice. The pith is sweet too, but was too valuable to chew.

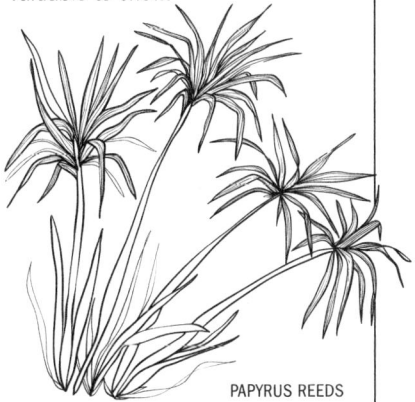

PAPYRUS REEDS

Though papyrus was once abundant throughout the Nile Delta in northern Egypt, it's nearly impossible to find anywhere in the country today. When other products replaced papyrus for papermaking, Egyptians stopped planting and harvesting the reeds. Papyrus grows farther south now, in Central Africa, closer to where the Nile River begins.

CHILDBIRTH IN ANCIENT EGYPT

NO MEN ALLOWED

People who lived in Egypt enjoyed some of the best healthcare available at the time. Papyrus documents report that Egypt had physicians who specialized in many fields. There were eye doctors, foot doctors, stomach doctors.

But there were no doctors who delivered babies.

That was women's business, left to midwives—like Shiphrah and Puah—for people who could afford them. Poorer women would turn to a village elder lady or to a mother, sister, or another female relative or friend.

A good midwife had "long, slim fingers and short nails at her fingertips," according to Roman physician Soranus (AD 98–138), writing a book called *Gynecology*.

BIRTHING STOOLS AND BRICKS

Roman writers more than a millennium after Moses described details of a delivery. But archaeologists say they haven't found any Egyptian descriptions yet.

They do say that pictures show Egyptian women delivering their babies sitting squatted on either a birthing chair or two large bricks. This position let midwives take advantage of gravity to help in the delivery.

Egyptologist Joseph Wegner reported discovering a 3,700-year-old birthing brick in the ruins of an Egyptian mayor's house. Someone had painted the mud brick with colorful religious pictures. Wegner suggests Egyptians considered birth a religious event. One scene on the brick shows a mother and her baby accompanied by Hathor, a cow goddess Egyptians linked to birth and childcare. Wegner said the top of the brick was worn and crumbling from use.

TEMPLE WALL RELIEF FROM KOM OMBO

WHAT'S IN A NAME:
MOSES

◆

"The princess named him Moses, for she explained, 'I lifted him out of the water." (Exodus 2:10 NLT) In fact, his name in Hebrew, Mosheh (mo-SHAY) sounds a little like Hebrew for "lift" or "drew out," mashah (maw-SHAW).

But to Egyptians, the name comes from a verb that means "son of"...who knows. Thutmose meant "son of Thut," referring to Thoth, the god who maintained the universe. At least ten pharaohs shared the name "mose."

Moses, on the other hand, was simply "son of..." who knows. Had Egyptians tagged him to the Hebrew God, they might have called him Yahmose, short for "son of Yahweh," God of Israel.

HIGH INFANT MORTALITY RATE

Childbirth and childhood were dangerous. Approximately one-third of all babies born in ancient Egypt died within a few months of birth, and nearly half did not reach adulthood.

King Tut experienced this tragedy twice. His two tiny daughters were buried with him in his tomb. Neither had survived birth. One was born about three months premature. A full-term daughter died at birth.

WET NURSES: WHEN BABY NEEDS MORE

Some new moms in ancient Egypt, like today, couldn't produce enough milk for their baby.

Other moms were trying to breastfeed more than one baby at a time, since breastfeeding in ancient Egypt could go on for several years. The two-year-old needs Mommy and so does the newborn.

Tragically, there were many moms who didn't survive labor. That left their babies with nothing at all to eat.

For all these babies, getting milk was a matter of life or death. It wasn't just a matter of convenience, for royalty and for the rich elite who didn't want to bother breastfeeding.

Yet when a queen or a princess in Egypt gave birth, her baby often went directly to a respected and vetted wet nurse. Wet nurses got a status boost because of the work they did. Some show up on ancient guest lists at royal events.

RATING THE BREAST MILK

Connoisseurs of breast milk in ancient Egypt rated the quality of the milk on the aroma. Egyptians said the best breast milk smelled like "powder of manna," whatever that meant. The Bible says manna tasted sweet, "like wafers with honey" (Exodus 16:31 NASB). Egyptians said bad milk tasted like fish.

Oddly enough, though, when a wet nurse started producing poor-quality breast milk, one of the treatments involved rubbing her back with fish-scented oil and reciting incantations.

IDEAL WET NURSE

When Egyptians looked for a wet nurse, like Moses' mother Jochebed (called Kebi in our story), these are some of the qualities they wanted to see, and the reasons they gave.

- **Unmarried (widowed or divorced).** It was believed that currently celibate women produced better breast milk.
- **No babies of her own.** Feeding children other than the one she was hired to feed diminished milk quality.
- **Sticks to assigned diet.** Wet nurse's food affected baby's food.
- **Has a son beyond breastfeeding age.** Some Egyptians valued the milk of a woman who had given birth to a son. It was a man's world.

WHO ARE THE PHARAOHS OF JOCHEBED'S TIME?

DIGGING FOR TRUTH: THE SEARCH FOR A PHARAOH

As mentioned in the introduction to this book, the date of the Exodus is hotly contested among scholars. So is the identity of the pharaohs surrounding the Exodus narrative.

No one has turned up conclusive evidence to ID which pharaoh had a princess-daughter who raised Moses. Was it Akhenaten, as the author suggests, or someone else? If we want to solve that mystery, it seems some archaeologists are going to have to grab a shovel and go dig some more.

KING TUT

What they need to find first is one piece of evidence that puts Moses on the calendar. Outside the Bible, there's no mention of him. Many history scholars say he's more legend than human—a composite of leaders or a collection of imaginary stories. But many also said the same of King David until his name showed up in 1993, chiseled into stone nearly 3,000 years ago: "king of the House of David."

Second, after someone unearths a record of Moses in the sand, they need to find something to settle scholarly dustups over when the pharaohs ruled some 3,500 years ago. Scholars argue over many of those dates from around the time Moses lived.

THE NUMBERS GAME: HUNTING PHARAOH WITH MATH

We'll do the math, but we shouldn't get our hopes up.

Option 1, go with Solomon. We start our hunt for the pharaoh with Solomon and then work back to Baby Moses. "During the fourth year of Solomon's reign [about 960 BC] . . . he began to construct the Temple of the LORD. This was 480 years after the people of Israel were rescued from their slavery in the land of Egypt" (1 Kings 6:1 NLT).

That puts Moses at the front of the line of Hebrews leaving Egypt in

251

about 1440 BC, when "Moses was eighty years old" (Exodus 7:7 NLT).

Eighty plus 1440 is his birth date: 1520 BC. The problem? No one knows who the pharaoh was then.

Dates of three Egyptian rulers in the low-numbered 1500s BC are all disputed by decades: Ahmose I, Amenhotep I, Thutmose I, and Thutmose II.

Option 2, go with Rameses. "Egyptians made the Israelites their slaves. . . . They forced them to build the cities of Pithom and Rameses as supply centers for the king" (Exodus 1:11 NLT).

Rameses II, the famous builder king of Egypt, ruled from 1279–1213 BC. To estimate when Moses led the Hebrews in the Exodus out of Egypt, let's shoot for a round number near the middle of Rameses's reign, 1250 BC. That assumes Rameses was smart enough not to lead his army into the parted seawater that collapsed "and covered all the chariots and charioteers—the entire army of Pharaoh" (Exodus 14:28 NLT).

Eighty plus 1250 is 1330 BC, when Moses may have been born.

Hello, eleven-year-old King Tut. Young Tutankhamun (born about 1341 BC, died about 1323 BC) was the son of Pharaoh Akhenaten. Tut ruled from about 1332–1323 BC, give or take a year or two. If Moses had been born anytime during King Tut's reign, Tut would have been little more than a kid. He died at around age 18 or 19.

If the Exodus out of Egypt took place earlier in the reign of Rameses, Moses could have been born during the reign of Tut's father, Akhenaten—husband of the famously gorgeous Nefertiti. Akhenaten is the pharaoh who tried to convince Egyptians to worship one god, Aten, represented by pictures of the sun disc. While

AKHENATEN

some historians say they wonder if this influenced Moses toward belief in one God, many Bible scholars say it was God Himself who influenced Moses, beginning with a burning bush.

Akhenaten (aka Amenhotep IV) had six daughters, each one a princess who might have taken a bath in the Nile and discovered a baby boy floating in a basket.

THE FIERCE NILE CROCODILE

Meanest, biggest, ugliest ambush predator anyone or anything wandering near the Nile River would never want to bump into—that's the Nile crocodile, considered the most vicious of all crocodile species.

The Nile crocodile eats mostly fish. But it will kill and eat sheep, cattle, and people too. Even today, these crocs reportedly kill hundreds of people each year.

Full-grown, a Nile crocodile can stretch about 16 feet long (5 meters) and weigh half a ton or more, up to about 1,500 pounds.

They're huge. But put them in water and they can swim four times faster than any Olympic champion swimmer. Crocodile max speed: 22 mph (35 km/h), compared to a 50-meter-freestyle champion chugging along at a comparatively modest 5.3 mph (8.6 km/h).

Egyptians linked crocodiles to a god called Sobek, revered as a deity who could strengthen an army and improve fertility in families, flocks, and fields.

At times, some scholars say, Egyptians probably worshipped a crocodile as a living, crawling, snapping incarnation of Sobek.

Egyptians mummified some crocodiles. A 3-D scan of a 2,500-year-old crocodile mummy in 2016 revealed two adolescent crocodiles with 47 individually wrapped baby crocodiles. This may have been a sacrificial gift for a recently departed Sobek incarnation croc to enjoy in the afterlife.

Some scholars speculate that the Nile crocodile, which once lived along Israel's coast, may have been the mysterious Leviathan monster of the Bible. "Can you catch Leviathan with a hook…?…The scales on its back are like rows of shields tightly sealed together" (Job 41:1, 15 NLT).

Fiction Author
CAROLE TOWRISS

An unapologetic Californian, Carole Towriss now lives just north of Washington, DC. She loves her husband, her four children, the beach, and tacos, though not always in that order. In addition to writing, Carole binge-watches British crime dramas and does the dishes for the fourth time in one day.

Nonfiction Author
STEPHEN M. MILLER

Stephen M. Miller is an award-winning, bestselling Christian author of easy-reading books about the Bible and Christianity.

His books have sold over 1.9 million copies and include *The Complete Guide to the Bible, Who's Who and Where's Where in the Bible,* and *How to Get into the Bible.*

Stephen lives in the suburbs of Kansas City with his wife, Linda, a registered nurse. They have two married children who live nearby.

Read on for a sneak peek of another exciting story in the Ordinary Women of the Bible series!

✦

THE HEALER'S TOUCH: TIKVA'S STORY

by Connilyn Cossette

A mischievous gust of wind whipped Tikva's white headscarf from its mooring. The linen flapped and danced around her like the wings of a tethered dove. With a laugh, she snatched the fabric from the air before it flew out to sea. If only it could drift over the restless waters, search out the one vessel Tikva longed to see, and guide it home. It seemed like years since her Asa had been at sea. Five months was far too long without her husband.

The crash of waves at the foot of the bluff where she stood misted salty droplets over her skin. Breathing in the cool freshness of the ocean breeze, she replaced her headscarf, tucking it securely about her neck and drawing it over her forehead, a buffer against the sparkling glare. Squinting, she continued to peer at the horizon, willing a dark shape to break the line between sky and sea.

She wondered whether she'd ever get used to the tides of life with a man who made his living on the Great Sea. Helena, her husband's mother, had warned her not to stop at the bluff on the way home from the market, saying that the wait would only be prolonged by obsessively watching the horizon for signs of his return—but still, Tikva came, tipping up on her toes and shading her eyes to scan the distance, praying that Adonai would guide Asa's ship home to Ptolemais with all speed. As the wife of a man who traded far across the expanse, to lands she could barely imagine, she knew she must learn to wait patiently. But surely one could forgive a young bride her anxiety during this first separation. Helena may shake her head and cluck at her daughter-in-law's wringing hands, but Tikva guessed that many years ago it had been Helena standing on this same bluff every afternoon, waiting for Asa's father to slide into port.

Placing a hand on the burgeoning curve of her belly, Tikva repeated her husband's name, hoping that the wind would bear her prayers aloft, straight to the ears of the Almighty. A flutter beneath her palm was the only answer, a silent agreement from the life within that Asa must return as soon as possible. How Tikva longed to see the look on his face when he beheld the mound beneath her tunic, since neither of them had known she was with child five months before when he boarded his ship!

She stroked her fingers across the swell of her middle, dreaming of the day it would be the sweet head of an infant her fingers would caress instead. Would the babe have Asa's deep blue eyes inherited from his Greek mother? His long nose and his sailor's build? Or would he mimic Tikva with her black curls and brown eyes? Asa had talked of little more than a son since their marriage only eight months before, and she longed to place an heir into his arms.

Another swirl of wind tugged at Tikva's skirt, dodging around her ankles like a playful pup, whipping her hair across her eyes. The ocean dipped and swayed, foaming white as it heaved itself against the rocks. She tried not to imagine what the waves might look like far past the breakwater, out beyond the dark clouds that painted the northern sky, nor to remember the tales her father-in-law loved to tell about the fearsome creatures that haunted the deep.

A sprinkle of rain dashed across her cheek, cutting short her vigil. She slipped her market basket higher on her forearm and tucked it close to her body, unwilling to allow the honey cakes she'd purchased from an Egyptian vendor to come to ruin in the sudden rain shower, then plodded down the hill toward the two patient maidservants who waited near the bottom.

Her mother-in-law would shake her head and purse her lips when she returned soaked to the skin, but one of these afternoons Tikva would glimpse a tiny dot on the horizon, one that would grow and grow until her Asa was back in her embrace, and a few gusts of wind and a little rain would mean nothing at all.

◆

"And where have you been?" Helena said the moment Tikva entered the house, as if they did not have this conversation at least twice a week. Although deep into preparations for the Shabbat meal, her light brown hair in a frazzled halo about her face, her mother-in-law was never too busy supervising to chide.

"The market and then the bluff," said Tikva, handing her the basket of the Egyptian honey cakes that she knew Helena was so fond of.

Helena shook her head, mouth pursed as she examined the contents of the basket with not a word of thanks. "It's time to end these excursions, Tikva. You have your babe to consider now. Watching the horizon will not make him return any sooner."

Tikva slid a protective hand over her belly. "I did not exert myself overmuch, I assure you. I would not risk Asa's child for anything."

Helena's glare softened at the name of her precious son. "Be that as it may, you have no need to go to the market, especially on Preparation Day. Too many people milling about. Let Mina and Dara tend to the shopping alone next time."

"I enjoy going with them," Tikva said. "I love to see what new goods have come into port and meeting people from all over the world. Today there was a merchant with linen straight from Egypt, along with the most beautiful turquoise I've ever seen. And the—"

Helena patted her hand, cutting off the description of the wonders Tikva had discovered in the market. "I know you are restless, young as you are. But once the little one comes, you'll have more than enough to fill your time. Now, why don't you go rest for a while until your father and mother arrive? You must not over tire yourself." She handed the basket of rolls to Mina, gesturing for the Phoenician girl to take the treats outside to the kitchen courtyard before swirling off to direct the placement of the flowers that had been gathered from her extensive and well-tended gardens. Helena ran her household with great skill, her servants so attuned to her every wish that she needn't even speak aloud her wishes for them to be fulfilled.

And someday I'll be the mistress of this grand household. The idea thrilled Tikva as much as it made her uneasy. As the daughter of one of the leaders of the synagogue, she'd been by no means poverty stricken, but her father-in-law was one of the wealthiest merchants in Ptolemais. This house was twice the size of the one she'd been born into, with at least ten servants tending to her every need. Tikva had lived here now for the past eight months, since she and Asa had married, but sometimes she still felt like an interloper, one who contributed little to the household at that.

Helena was right that she'd be glad for the babe to be born, not only because she'd be providing Asa with the child he so desperately wanted but because she'd have more to do than wander through the house, wishing he were there. Perhaps when Shabbat was over she would visit Lilah and Margalit, her cousins and closest friends. She'd not seen them for weeks and was desperate for someone her own age with whom she could speak freely.

Unlike Helena, Tikva's mother had insisted she always keep her hands busy when she'd lived at home: cooking, sewing, and cleaning. Her *imma* regarded idleness with nearly as much disdain as she did the beggars that huddled near the gates of the city. Tikva hoped that when her family came for the meal tonight, her mother would not ask what she'd been doing to make herself useful to Helena, because she had no answer.

At least the beggars outside the gates filled their days with the occupation of raising their filthy hands to passersby and lifting their voices to demand alms. Here she was in the way of the bustling servants more often than not, and since Tikva had realized she was with child just after Asa's ship departed, Helena complained anytime she spent more than a few minutes on her feet. As if a short walk through the city and then up a small incline would strip her body of strength.

Annoyed with Helena's overprotectiveness and thankful that, although the day continued to be gray, the rain shower had passed, Tikva slipped out the back door and up the slick stairs to the rooftop, trading hours of lying on her plush bed in boredom for the fresh breeze and the narrow strip of sea view she could snatch between neighboring buildings. It was not the bluff, where the entire blue expanse spread out before her, but it was better than nothing. She pulled a tall stool over to the parapet and sat with her elbows on the wet stone wall. Then, chin in hand, she took up her vigil, glad that at least this evening her loneliness would be buffered by the presence of her mother and father at the Shabbat meal.

◆

Oil lamps flickered along the length of the table, highlighting the array of lovely dishes Helena's cooks had prepared.

Herb-encrusted roasted dove and spicy goat stew lent the room a delicious odor while a vast array of fruits, cheeses, varicolored olives, and freshly baked bread caused Tikva's belly to rumble with anticipation.

Of course, before they could partake in this lovely feast, a blessing must be offered. So with hands outstretched, Tikva's father stood at the head of the table, his deep voice resonant as he recited the familiar words of gratitude to the Ruler of the Universe who created all and sustained all. When, at last, his copious blessings over the food and drink were complete, and he finally folded himself down to recline at the table, Mina and Dara padded into the room to fill everyone's cups with wine.

"Rabbi Shmuel, I am so glad you and Naomi accepted our invitation to join us for the Shabbat meal this evening," said Helena. "I'd hoped that Nachman and Asa would be here to partake with us, but hopefully it will not be much longer before their ship arrives in port."

Tikva's father nodded as he lifted a bite to his lips, barely acknowledging Helena as she spoke. Tikva remembered a time when her father had been effusive with his compliments and smiled widely at men and women alike, but as his status had risen within the synagogue he'd become more and more careful to limit his interactions with those not of his own sex. As a Pharisee, one with a fair amount of influence within Ptolemais and its surrounding areas, he'd become diligent in his observance of the Law, both written and oral, and had taken to heart the admonishments of the learned rabbis against familiarity with women not of his family.

At least he was not like some of his counterparts, who insisted on crossing the street when women came into view, in the off-chance that one of them might be ritually unclean during their monthly time, but still, his slight against Helena, who'd worked so hard to organize such a plentiful table in his honor, grated against Tikva's nerves.

Thankfully, he did not include Tikva in such convictions, even though she was a married woman and no longer a part of his household. As Helena and Tikva discussed the lovely new kidskin sandals her mother had purchased, Tikva's father leaned closer to her, a small smile on his lips.

"Your mother informs me you are with child, Daughter."

"I am," she replied.

"I am pleased to hear it," he said, and her heart trembled with pleasure at his obvious pride. "Perhaps you will fulfill your duty and provide Asa with an heir even before Shavuot next year."

"Yes, Abba. That would be wonderful. Although a daughter would be most pleasant as well." She knew a son was expected of her, and prayed for by her husband, but she did long for a little girl to cherish.

"And just think, your son will inherit all of this," said her father, with a sweep of his palm around the richly appointed room. "Nachman has built quite a reputation in his dealings with Cyprus and Rome, I can imagine that his business will thrive in the years to come. Asa, too, is a shrewd merchant, like his father. He will pass on quite a legacy to your little one. I knew I made the right choice of husband for you."

She blinked at him, confused by the statement that contradicted her memory. "But did not Asa seek you out first? After he met me outside the synagogue during Shavuot?"

He furrowed his dark brows in confusion. "No. His father and I brokered an agreement years ago. He donated funds toward the new synagogue in exchange for your hand, and therefore my goodwill. He is not a fool, Tikva. He knows that we rabbis hold the ear of the people in this city. His continuing contributions to our coffers are certainly welcome, and we've ensured that his name is held in high regard in this region."

Confusion swirled in Tikva's mind. Asa had told her that he'd been enthralled by her beauty that day and had not rested until his father approached hers to beg for a betrothal. And yet it seemed she had been nothing but a bargaining tool between her father and Nachman instead.

"How fortunate that you've fallen pregnant so soon. It will ensure the connection is strong between us for years to come."

A pang of deep hurt pressed between her ribs. It seemed her father considered the life within her womb as much of a commodity as her own.

Her father smiled as he reached to place a hand atop her head. "I am proud of you, daughter. You have done so well." Then he lifted his voice again, to pray a blessing over her and the child who'd fulfilled his wishes before it had even taken a breath.

Her mother and Helena looked on with undisguised pride as well, both of them just as thrilled as her father that Tikva had done her duty to their respective families.

As the rain pattered hard against the shutters, Tikva prayed once again for Asa to come home, not only to wrap her in his arms and chase away the loneliness but to reassure her that he had chosen her as his wife, that he'd offered for her hand because he cared for her, and not purchased her to ensure security for his trade in Ptolemais.

◆

If you'd like to read the rest of this thrilling story, *The Healer's Touch: Tikva's Story* by Connilyn Cossette, visit: shopguideposts.org to sign up for the series or purchase the individual book.